Are We Alone in This Universe?

Are We Alone in This Universe?

Vinu V Das

Tabor Press

ISBN 978-1-997541-13-4

Table of Contents

Chapter 1: The Grand Question of Cosmic Existence

The question "Are we alone in this universe?" has stirred human imagination for millennia. From ancient civilizations that looked to the stars as divine symbols, to modern-day astronomy probing the depths of space, the search for cosmic companions has remained constant. Whether spurred by a sense of awe, scientific inquiry, or theological reflection, people yearn to know if life extends beyond Earth's borders. In Christian contexts, this question intersects with profound truths about God as the Creator, the purpose of humanity, and the scope of redemption.

1.1. A Sense of Wonder

1.1.1 Humanity's Enduring Curiosity

The Innate Drive to Explore

From the earliest cave dwellers who painted celestial shapes on their walls, humanity has exhibited a primal curiosity about what lies beyond the immediate horizon. This curiosity propels our collective growth. It sparks the invention of the telescope, the launching of satellites, and the writing of countless myths and theories. Though culture and technology have changed, the instinct to peer into the unknown remains fundamentally the same.

When we gaze at the night sky, we confront our own smallness in a cosmos that seems to stretch infinitely in every direction. This awareness produces a mixture of humility and exhilaration—an emotional blend that has been both unsettling and inspiring. Children staring up at the stars for the first time often ask, "What's out there?" That innocent question resonates with scientists, theologians, and philosophers who devote their lives to the pursuit of answers.

Yet even before the complexities of formal science came into play, humanity's curiosity about life beyond Earth was rooted in daily observations—patterns in the sky, phases of the moon, shifting constellations across seasons. Ancient navigators used the stars to guide sea voyages, revealing not only a practical application of cosmic knowledge but also a sense of reverence for the heavens as a reliable guide. Over time, this practical relationship with the sky grew into more speculative inquiries: If our own planet teems with life, might not other celestial bodies do the same?

Philosophical Questions and Yearnings

Beyond observational curiosity, there is an existential weight to these questions. For instance, the Greek philosophers of antiquity considered whether the visible cosmos was eternal or created, whether it was single or made up of multiple worlds, and whether gods or other beings populated it. Though such philosophical discussions were not shaped by modern scientific methods, they grappled with the same sense of wonder that causes us to reflect on the possibility of extraterrestrial neighbors.

In contemporary times, we may be armed with advanced technology and a deeper scientific understanding of cosmic scales. Still, the underlying philosophical hunger remains.

Faith traditions around the world—Christianity, Judaism, Islam, Hinduism, Buddhism—have each sought to answer fundamental questions about humanity's relationship to the universe. While the answers differ, the motivation is universal: a desire to know our place and to understand the overarching narrative that ties the cosmos together.

The Christian tradition particularly emphasizes that humans, created in the "image of God" (Genesis 1:26), possess an inherent drive to search out the wonders of creation. Curiosity, therefore, is not merely an accident of evolution or a quirk of psychology but can be seen as part of what it means to be made in the divine image. The biblical mandate in Genesis 1:28, where humankind is instructed to "fill the earth and subdue it," suggests an encouragement toward exploration and stewardship—an invitation to discover and caret for God's creation, both near and far.

Emotional Resonance

Curiosity also evokes emotional dimensions: it is not only an intellectual quest but a deeply felt experience. The thrill of standing under a star-filled sky, the tranquil humility of peering at distant galaxies through a telescope—these moments affect us at our core. They can stir spiritual awareness, leading us to sense the presence of something greater than ourselves. When we ask, "Are we alone?" we are not just probing a scientific puzzle; we are also asking about meaning, about whether our story intersects with a cosmic drama that extends beyond humanity.

Such emotional resonance drives the creative expressions of poets, artists, and musicians. For centuries, sacred music and art have incorporated celestial imagery to capture the majesty of God's realm. This underscores how curiosity about life beyond Earth can be a pathway into deeper worship and reverence. It reminds believers that our God is not a provincial deity but the Lord of a universe filled with wonders yet to be understood (Psalm 8:3-4).

1.1.2 Cultural Perspectives on Cosmic Life

Ancient Myths and Legends

The question of cosmic existence—particularly whether other beings occupy the heavens—appears in numerous ancient myths. Civilizations such as the Babylonians, Egyptians, Chinese, and Mayans left records reflecting beliefs that the stars and planets were inhabited by gods or ancestral spirits. Tales of beings descending from the sky to communicate with humans or to shape historical events abound in early literature.

These myths served multiple functions. They provided a framework for understanding natural phenomena like meteor showers or solar eclipses. They also reinforced communal identity by linking a tribe's origin story to celestial happenings. Even though Christians do not accept these myths as literal truth, they stand as a testament to humanity's persistent fascination with what lies beyond. Notably, the biblical account of creation does not present the sun, moon, or stars as deities, contrary to many neighboring cultures of ancient Israel. Instead, Genesis 1:16 demystifies these celestial bodies by simply calling them "the greater light" and "the lesser light," thus establishing a worldview where they are creations rather than creators.

Medieval and Renaissance Views

The Middle Ages in Europe saw a shift toward a more hierarchical understanding of the cosmos, influenced significantly by the works of Aristotle and Ptolemy. In such models, Earth was the center of creation, surrounded by concentric celestial spheres. Even though these theories were not specifically Christian but philosophical, they often merged with Christian teachings on cosmic order.

While many believed angels populated the heavens, the notion of physical extraterrestrial life was less commonly discussed, though not entirely absent. Artistic depictions of heaven, saints, and angels in the medieval period sometimes depicted swirling cosmic backgrounds, offering subtle hints that the heavens were teeming with realities beyond mere empty space. Later, with the onset of the Renaissance, figures like Nicolaus Copernicus and Galileo Galilei began to challenge geocentric views, fueling speculation about the possibility of other inhabited worlds—a curiosity that would blossom in subsequent centuries.

Modern Pop Culture and Media

In the modern era, science fiction literature, television, and cinema have exploded with imaginative portrayals of alien civilizations. These cultural artifacts often reflect both excitement and anxiety about meeting life from other worlds. Themes of invasion, cooperation, technological marvels, and spiritual awakenings are woven into these narratives. While not necessarily rooted in biblical worldview, they offer insight into how broader society grapples with the question of cosmic community.

Interestingly, some Christian thinkers have engaged with these pop-culture portrayals, seeing them as a new way to ask time-honored questions: If an alien civilization exists, do they share in our moral and spiritual struggles? Are they part of the same salvation history? Although these questions will be addressed in more depth in later parts of the book, it is worth noting here that popular media exemplifies just how embedded the question of cosmic existence has become in contemporary consciousness.

Common Threads Across Cultures

Despite the diversity of expressions—myths, religious texts, philosophical treatises, modern media—certain themes consistently recur. First, there is a recognition of humanity's limited knowledge compared to the vast expanse of creation. Second, there is a longing for connection with a realm beyond our immediate experience. Third, there is a mix of apprehension and hope that contact with "others" would fundamentally change our self-understanding.

These recurring themes underscore how integral the question of cosmic existence is to human identity. Whether one stands in a medieval cathedral or a modern observatory, the sense of wonder is palpable. Our gaze upward unites us, inviting us to see ourselves not in isolation, but as participants in a drama that may stretch far beyond Earth. This is where Christian faith brings a unique lens: the God who made the heavens and the earth (Genesis 1:1) is, from a biblical perspective, intimately concerned with human life—even while presiding over a vast universe whose full scope we have yet to comprehend.

1.2. Biblical Foundations of Creation

1.2.1 "In the Beginning": A Cosmic Scope

The Opening Verses of Genesis

"In the beginning, God created the heavens and the earth" (Genesis 1:1). These are arguably the most famous opening words of any text. Though often read through the lens of Earth-bound concerns, the phrase "the heavens and the earth" immediately places creation in a cosmic frame. It is not merely a localized story about a single planet in isolation; the biblical writer deliberately paints the stage of an expansive theater, the full scope of which remains mysterious.

Genesis is not a scientific treatise. It uses figurative language, repetition, and a particular structure to communicate theological truths: God is the Creator, creation is purposeful, and humanity has a special place within it. Yet even so, the cosmic perspective emerges strongly. Biblical scholars have noted that the Hebrew word for "heavens" (shamayim) can encompass not just the atmosphere or sky but the totality of the cosmic expanse. Modern readers may call this universe, cosmos, or space. The point is that from the very first sentence, Scripture invites us to recognize that God's handiwork is profoundly bigger than our immediate surroundings.

The Scope of Creation in Other Passages

Genesis 1:16 states, "God made the two great lights—the greater light to rule the day and the lesser light to rule the night—and the stars." The casual mention of the stars seems almost understated by modern standards, given that contemporary science reveals hundreds of billions of stars in our galaxy alone, and potentially trillions of galaxies beyond. Yet this mention underscores the biblical worldview that everything in the night sky, from the nearest planet to the most distant galaxy, owes its existence to God's creative power.

Elsewhere, biblical writers echo this cosmic scope. For example, Psalm 33:6 declares, "By the word of the Lord the heavens were made, and by the breath of his mouth all their host." The term "host" implies a vast array—an innumerable assembly. While the ancient psalmist certainly did not have a modern conception of galaxies or exoplanets, the language nevertheless pushes the reader to imagine something grander than a simple, flat sky.

Isaiah 40:26 admonishes, "Lift up your eyes on high and see: who created these? He who brings out their host by number, calling them all by name." Again, the text suggests that God's domain includes not just our immediate environment but an immense celestial order. The repeated command to "lift your eyes on high" indicates that Scripture itself compels believers to look beyond earthly boundaries, implicitly validating the quest to understand the broader cosmos.

Implications for Cosmic Inquiry

If Scripture provides a cosmic vantage point from its opening lines, then wondering about life beyond Earth is not an alien pursuit but a natural extension of biblical curiosity. Rather than confine our focus to terrestrial matters alone, Scripture places humanity within a grand framework that includes countless stars and potentially even more wonders that remain unseen. This does not necessarily mean the Bible teaches the existence of extraterrestrial life. But it does mean that the biblical worldview, at its core, allows for a universe of significant scale and complexity—a universe worthy of exploration, both scientifically and theologically.

For Christians, this cosmic perspective can cultivate both humility and reverence. We see ourselves as cherished by God, yet we also recognize that we occupy a small corner of an immense creation. Instead of diminishing the significance of faith, this recognition can magnify it: the God who is mindful of our daily concerns (Psalm 8:4) is also the God who set galaxies in motion. Such an understanding lays a theological foundation for asking whether other planets might host life—and how that might fit into God's broader purposes.

Resonance with Ancient and Contemporary Minds

It is striking that, although the ancient Hebrews lacked modern astronomical tools, their writings in Genesis and elsewhere resonate with modern discoveries about the vastness of space. This does not imply that the biblical authors were "ahead of their time" in a literal scientific sense, but rather that their theological imagination was expansive. They recognized that God's creativity likely extends beyond human comprehension.

Today, astrophysicists use advanced telescopes to confirm that the universe is incredibly large—potentially much larger than we can observe. Meanwhile, the biblical text remains unthreatened by each new discovery. In fact, new cosmic findings often reinforce the sense of awe the ancient authors captured in their praise of the Creator. Thus, the earliest pages of Scripture already situate the faithful reader in a mindset of cosmic wonder, affirming that big questions about existence beyond Earth align comfortably with biblical faith.

1.2.2 Heaven and Earth: A Dual Reality

Understanding "Heaven" in Biblical Context

The term "heaven" (or "the heavens") in the Bible carries layers of meaning. On one level, it refers to the visible sky where birds fly and clouds form. On another level, it represents the vast cosmic realm of stars and celestial bodies. There is also a spiritual dimension: "heaven" sometimes denotes the dwelling place of God, where angels worship (Psalm 148:2). These meanings can overlap in subtle ways, making it essential for readers to consider context when interpreting references to "heaven" in Scripture.

In many Old Testament narratives, heaven appears as a realm intimately connected to Earth. Blessings and judgments come "down from heaven," reflecting the idea that all good things ultimately come from God above. At the same time, heaven is a place beyond ordinary human access, reinforcing the notion that the divine realm transcends earthly limitations. Yet, passages like 1 Kings 8:27 acknowledge that "even heaven and the highest heaven cannot contain" God, suggesting that God is beyond even the cosmic expanse.

Earth as Humanity's Primary Abode

While Scripture begins by announcing the creation of "the heavens and the earth," it also focuses intensely on Earth as the stage for human life, moral development, and redemption. The biblical drama, from Genesis to Revelation, unfolds primarily on this planet, with particular attention to the people of Israel in the Old Testament and the global Church in the New Testament era. This Earth-centric narrative does not negate the possibility of life elsewhere; rather, it reflects the perspective of a text written to guide humanity's relationship with God.

Earth is repeatedly described as a place of divine-human interaction, from the Garden of Eden (Genesis 2) to the new creation of Revelation 21–22. This does not necessarily shut out the rest of the cosmos from God's interest. Indeed, the existence of angelic beings suggests that the biblical worldview acknowledges non-human forms of life, though spiritual in nature. The question of biological extraterrestrial life is beyond the direct scope of these passages. However, the dual emphasis on heaven and earth demonstrates that Scripture is already thinking in broader categories than just one planet.

Points of Intersection

Several biblical episodes hint at heaven and earth intersecting in surprising ways. For example, the story of Jacob's ladder (Genesis 28:12) describes a vision of angels ascending and descending between heaven and earth, illustrating a reality in which the boundary between the earthly realm and the heavenly realm is permeable under God's authority. Likewise, texts describing the glory of the Lord filling the temple (2 Chronicles 7:1-2) suggest moments when the divine presence tangibly touches the physical world.

While these passages primarily address spiritual truths rather than scientific phenomena, they reinforce the notion that creation extends beyond human sight. If the spiritual realm can intersect with Earth, might other parts of the physical creation not also be in some form of relationship with God? This line of reasoning does not offer direct proof of extraterrestrial life; however, it does encourage believers not to limit God's sovereignty to terrestrial boundaries.

A Universe Open to Exploration

"In the beginning, God created the heavens and the earth" can be read as a door swung wide open to the vastness of creation. Rather than a closed system existing only for humanity, Scripture depicts a universe replete with both physical and spiritual dimensions. Historically, Christians have sometimes been cautious about speculating too freely on matters not explicitly detailed in Scripture. Yet the Bible's cosmic language and repeated admonitions to consider the works of God's hands (Job 37:14; Psalm 8:3) allow room for thoughtful inquiry.

The biblical concept of heaven and earth being interconnected in God's sovereignty invites a humble approach. Yes, Earth is the home base of the biblical story, but the cosmos itself is God's canvas. As modern astronomy continues to reveal the depth and breadth of that canvas, believers can maintain confidence that nothing lies beyond the Creator's scope. If God deemed the cosmos worth creating, perhaps that same

God deems the question of whether we are alone worth pondering.

Conclusion

The grand question of cosmic existence—"Are we alone in this universe?"—sits at the intersection of wonder, curiosity, and biblical faith. From humanity's earliest moments, we have looked upward and asked about our place among the stars. Cultural narratives, whether mythic or modern, underscore how universal this inquiry is. The Bible, through its opening pages, provides an expansive cosmic framework, one that affirms God's role as the Creator of all that exists, seen and unseen, known and unknown.

In these foundational texts, we find no immediate confirmation of extraterrestrial life; yet the invitation to explore and contemplate remains. By describing God's creation in cosmic terms, Scripture gives believers permission—even encouragement—to look beyond Earth for signs of God's handiwork. At the same time, Earth holds a prominent place within that creation, serving as the backdrop for the biblical storyline of redemption and relationship.

As we move forward in this book, the chapters that follow will build upon these foundational themes, each tackling a unique angle. Historical Christian perspectives, deeper scriptural explorations, scientific findings, philosophical reflections, and pastoral implications will round out the conversation. But the heartbeat of it all remains the same: the stirrings of wonder that prompt us to ask big questions about life, faith, and the possibility that other creatures in the cosmos are part of God's grand design.

Chapter 2: The Heavens Declare the Glory of God

The second chapter of our exploration delves into the deeply scriptural conviction that the universe itself—often summarized as "the heavens"—testifies to the grandeur, holiness, and creative power of God. When people look at shimmering stars, swirling galaxies in photographs, or even the vibrant hues of a sunset, many experience an innate sense of awe. From a Christian standpoint, this awe can be understood as a response to the revelation of God's glory through creation.

Though many of us have been fascinated by the cosmos since childhood, gazing at the night sky can be more than an idle pastime; it can become a portal to deeper faith. Here, we will see how biblical authors speak of the heavens as a universal choir singing praise to God, inviting us to join in that song. The theological and spiritual implications of this perspective are profound. They not only shape our worship but also affect how we approach questions about life in the universe—questions that inevitably arise in an age of rapidly advancing scientific discovery.

2.1. The Scriptural Vision of the Cosmos

2.1.1 Psalm 19 and the Majesty of the Heavens

The Context and Poetry of Psalm 19

Psalm 19 stands as one of the most iconic scriptural affirmations that the physical universe bears witness to its Creator. Written in a style that blends both hymn and wisdom literature, the psalm begins with the resounding statement: "The heavens declare the glory of God; the skies proclaim the work of his hands" (Psalm 19:1 NIV). Though relatively short, these words introduce a grand concept: creation itself is not silent. Rather, it communicates—albeit in a non-verbal manner—knowledge about God's greatness.

The first six verses of Psalm 19 focus on the cosmos as a form of natural revelation. Each day "pours forth speech," and each night "reveals knowledge," yet there is "no speech or language where their voice is not heard" (Psalm 19:2-3). This poetic language encapsulates the paradox that, while the heavens do not literally talk, they communicate something so universal that it transcends linguistic barriers. For the psalmist, the sun's course from one end of the sky to the other is akin to a bridegroom emerging in splendor, a daily spectacle proclaiming the brilliance of its Maker.

This motif of non-verbal communication challenges readers to consider how God can be made known outside the confines of spoken or written words. Though Psalm 19 later shifts focus to the written Law (verses 7-14), the opening section remains a pivotal reference for Christian theology regarding the intrinsic testimony of nature. In essence, Psalm 19 declares that the majesty of the created order reflects the majesty of the One who set it in motion.

Cosmic Revelation and Human Response

When the psalmist proclaims the heavens as proclaimers of divine glory, an implicit question arises: How should humans respond to this cosmic testimony? Far from advocating a mere scientific curiosity, the psalmic vision beckons believers to worship. Scripture often connects reflection on nature to an attitude of reverence and humility before God. Psalm 8, for instance, complements Psalm 19 by asking, "When I consider your heavens, the work of your fingers... what is mankind that you are mindful of them?" (Psalm 8:3-4). The rhetorical answer is that humanity, despite its smallness, holds a uniquely dignified status as caretakers of creation.

However, it is in Psalm 19 that we see the clearest statement about the heavens' role in divine self-disclosure. The cosmic display calls forth a sense of awe that leads many believers into deeper prayer or reflection. In this way, the natural world serves almost as a universal liturgy. While not everyone who beholds a sunrise may consciously acknowledge God, the psalmist implies that the beauty and order of the cosmos are there to be interpreted by anyone who opens their heart.

The believer who contemplates the grandeur of space—whether seen through a humble pair of binoculars or the awe-inspiring images of the Hubble telescope—stands in continuity with the psalmist's ancient wonder. This continuity crosses cultural and historical divides, suggesting that the impulse to see God's hand in cosmic splendor transcends the boundaries of time and geography. Indeed, from the vantage point of modern astronomy, the cosmos appears far larger and more mysterious than the psalmist could have envisioned. Yet, that only amplifies the sense of majesty reflected in those early words: "The heavens declare the glory of God."

Echoes in the New Testament

Though Psalm 19 is rooted in the Hebrew Scriptures, its theme resonates throughout the New Testament as well. The Apostle Paul, in Romans 1:19-20, argues that God's invisible attributes—his eternal power and divine nature—are clearly perceived through what has been made, so that humanity is "without excuse." This passage dovetails with the poetic imagery of Psalm 19, reinforcing the idea that creation itself bears a witness to the Creator. While Paul's emphasis is on humanity's moral accountability, the notion undergirding it is consistent: the visible universe speaks to an invisible reality.

Modern Christians who wrestle with scientific discoveries about distant galaxies, exoplanets, and cosmic phenomena can find in these texts a solid scriptural foundation. While neither Psalm 19 nor Romans 1 explicitly addresses extraterrestrial life, both affirm that the cosmos is saturated with meaning and that the search for understanding among the stars need not be divorced from the quest for God. Rather, it can become an extension of the worshipful gaze that Psalm 19 envisions.

2.1.2 Prophetic Imagery in Isaiah and Revelation

Isaiah's Cosmic Canvas

Where Psalm 19 uses poetic language to describe the heavens as proclaimers of God's glory, the prophet Isaiah employs cosmic imagery to highlight both God's transcendence and His covenant relationship with His people. Although Isaiah's prophecies center on Israel's moral and spiritual state, references to the grandeur of creation abound. Isaiah 40:22 portrays God as the one "who sits above the circle of the earth," reminding readers that the nations are like "grasshoppers" in comparison. The emphasis here is on God's unrivaled sovereignty. By presenting the earth's inhabitants as miniature relative to the vast canopy of the heavens, Isaiah accentuates the majestic scale of God's dominion.

Similarly, Isaiah 40:26 exhorts, "Lift up your eyes on high and see: who created these?" Here, the prophet's rhetorical style parallels the psalmic invitation to ponder the wonders of the sky. The difference lies in the context: Isaiah is addressing a people who have faced national calamity and exile, reassuring them that their covenant God remains omnipotent. The cosmic scope of God's power underscores His ability to redeem and restore. For a modern reader, these verses can function as a double encouragement: not only does the cosmos speak of God's greatness, but that greatness also undergirds His faithfulness toward His people.

Prophetic literature thus connects cosmic imagery with moral and spiritual realities. While the heavens might serve as a testament to God's creative might, they also remind believers that divine governance spans from the cosmic to the personal. That dual emphasis is crucial for any Christian grappling with questions of cosmic significance: God's authority is not just on display in swirling galaxies far away—it is also intimately relevant to human history and personal salvation.

Revelation's Visions of Cosmic Worship

Moving to the New Testament, the Book of Revelation brims with apocalyptic imagery that situates earthly events within a larger cosmic drama. Although much of Revelation employs symbolic language to convey its visions, the repeated references to celestial phenomena highlight a profound theme: the entire cosmos participates in or witnesses the unfolding plan of God. Revelation 4–5, for instance, presents the throne room of God, where creatures "in heaven and on earth and under the earth and in the sea, and all that is in them," join in a grand chorus of worship (Revelation 5:13). Though not a straightforward description of astronomy, this imagery suggests that worship is a cosmic affair, transcending terrestrial boundaries.

Revelation also employs cosmic signs to mark divine interventions or judgments (Revelation 6:12-14, 8:12). The sun darkening, stars falling from the sky, and the moon turning blood-red become symbols of dramatic shifts in redemptive history. Theologically, these metaphors communicate that the God who orchestrates salvation history is the same God who orders the heavens. For Christians wrestling with questions of life beyond Earth, such passages underscore the conviction that the cosmos is not a silent bystander to God's work but an integral part of a story that will culminate in what Revelation 21–22 describes as the renewal of "a new heaven and a new earth."

None of these texts definitively answer whether aliens exist. Nonetheless, they collectively suggest that the universe—and everything within it—ultimately serves to glorify God. In that sense, if life exists beyond Earth, it too would fall under the umbrella of God's creative and redemptive plan. In any case, the cosmic dimension of Revelation confirms that from a biblical perspective, the scope of divine glory extends far beyond human imagination, inviting wonder at the scale of God's handiwork.

2.2. Theological Implications

2.2.1 God's Transcendence and Immanence

Defining Transcendence

Within Christian theology, the term "transcendence" refers to God's existence beyond the limits of created reality. This means God is neither confined by spatial dimensions nor reducible to any cosmic structure. Such a perspective underscores the infinite gap between Creator and creation. Isaiah 55:8-9 captures this sentiment: "For my thoughts are not your thoughts, neither are your ways my ways... For as the heavens are higher than the earth, so are my ways higher than your ways." In linking the idea of divine transcendence to the heavens, the text draws a parallel between physical vastness and the immeasurable distance between finite humanity and an infinite God.

The cosmic images in Isaiah and Revelation, discussed above, reinforce this transcendence. While the heavens declare God's glory, they cannot contain Him. Indeed, 1 Kings 8:27 states that even "the highest heaven" cannot hold God's full presence. For believers pondering the enormity of the universe, divine transcendence reminds us that, no matter how large the cosmos is, God remains beyond and above its totality.

From the standpoint of curiosity about extraterrestrial life, transcendence suggests that God's relationship to the universe is not constrained by time, space, or biology. If creatures exist in distant galaxies, God is fully capable of knowing and sustaining them, just as He does with life on Earth. While Scripture focuses on earthly redemption narratives, transcendence implies that God's providential care need not be limited to a single planet. Rather, the same infinite God who created Earth's ecosystems could govern myriad worlds.

The Intimacy of Immanence

Yet biblical faith is not only about a distant, transcendent deity. Equally central is God's immanence—the conviction that God is actively present within creation. As Psalm 139:7-10 declares, there is nowhere one can flee from God's Spirit, neither in heaven nor in the depths of the sea. The God who sits enthroned above the circle of the earth (Isaiah 40:22) is also the God who knits each human being together in the womb (Psalm 139:13). This paradoxical blend of transcendence and immanence forms one of the core mysteries of Christian theology.

For those pondering cosmic life, immanence opens the possibility that God's sustaining presence permeates every corner of the universe. Even if humankind never encounters extraterrestrial beings, the principle of immanence suggests that no region of creation is spiritually neutral or devoid of the divine presence. In this sense, each star, planet, and galaxy exists within a God-infused context, whether or not they harbor living organisms.

Moreover, immanence fosters a sense of relational closeness. While transcendence might evoke worshipful awe, immanence encourages a confidence that God is intimately concerned with the details of creation—including the destiny of the human race and the potential existence of other races. It reassures believers that investigating the universe's mysteries is not an act of futility but an endeavor congruent with a faith that sees God intimately involved in every facet of reality.

Balancing Awe and Intimacy

Holding transcendence and immanence together can be challenging. Some might lean heavily on the grandeur of God, risking the impression that He is remote from everyday concerns. Others might emphasize divine nearness to the point of reducing God's majesty and authority. Biblical teaching, however, persistently keeps both attributes in tension. The heavens, in their splendor, evoke awe at God's magnitude. Simultaneously, the testimonies of prophets, psalmists, and apostles affirm that this grand God is near, as close as one's own breath.

In discussions of cosmic existence, balancing these two attributes helps prevent extremes. On one side, we avoid imagining a God who is locked away in a distant corner of the universe. On the other, we do not trivialize God's sovereignty by relegating Him to a "local deity" of Earth. Properly understood, transcendence fuels reverence, while immanence fosters trust—both of which are central to Christian worship, regardless of how wide the physical cosmos may stretch.

2.2.2 Creation's Order and Purpose

Biblical Themes of Order

Another key implication of the heavens declaring God's glory is the notion of cosmic order. Throughout the Old and New Testaments, creation is presented not as a chaotic accident but as an orderly design that reflects God's wisdom. Proverbs 8:27-29 personifies Wisdom and describes how God "marked out the foundations of the earth," setting boundaries and arranging the structures of the world. Similarly, Jeremiah 31:35 speaks of the "fixed order of the moon and the stars," suggesting that the very patterns of the skies are a testament to God's faithful governance.

Such biblical texts resonate with modern scientific discoveries about the fine-tuning of the universe. Scientists observe that the physical constants governing phenomena like gravity, electromagnetism, and nuclear forces appear precisely calibrated to permit life. While biblical authors did not use the language of cosmic constants or astrophysics, the underlying notion—that creation is purposeful and not haphazard—has deep scriptural roots. Every star, every planet, and every law of nature can thus be seen as part of a grand, divinely orchestrated design.

This perspective does not reduce the cosmic environment to a static, unchanging stage. Indeed, biblical narratives often describe creation as dynamic, subject to change or renewal. Nonetheless, overarching all variations is a coherent structure that points to a deliberate Mind behind it. The heavens, with their regular cycles and breathtaking complexity, illustrate this principle clearly: they are not random lights but part of an ordered system. For the Christian, that system proclaims, day after day, the wisdom and majesty of its Architect.

Humanity's Role Within Creation

The purposeful ordering of creation also raises questions about humanity's role, especially in light of potential extraterrestrial life. While Scripture unequivocally affirms humankind's significance, declaring humanity to be made in the image of God (Genesis 1:26-27), it does so within a context that acknowledges a vast universe. The tension—how can humans be both significant and relatively small—finds partial resolution in the concept of vocation. Humanity is tasked with cultivating and stewarding the Earth (Genesis 2:15), acting as representatives or vice-regents of God's reign over creation.

From this vantage point, discovering life elsewhere would not necessarily negate humanity's importance. Instead, it might expand our understanding of how creation's order extends beyond Earth. If God's design is as expansive as many suspect, our role could be seen as part of a broader cosmic tapestry. Though Scripture does not spell out how such a scenario would unfold, the principle of stewardship reminds us that we are neither passive observers nor self-appointed masters, but caretakers of what ultimately belongs to God.

Furthermore, the biblical vision of a renewed creation—a "new heaven and a new earth" (Revelation 21:1)—suggests that God's redemptive plan encompasses the entire cosmos. Even if we remain uncertain about whether alien life exists, this cosmic scope encourages us to view the universe with respect and wonder. The heavens do not merely function as an empty backdrop for human drama; they are part of a larger narrative of divine order and purpose, to be renewed and reconciled under God's sovereignty (Colossians 1:20).

Moral and Spiritual Order

Biblical notions of cosmic order also carry moral and spiritual implications. The same God who arranged the stars in their courses calls humanity to uphold ethical norms of justice, mercy, and holiness. The Scriptures often link the stability of the cosmic order to moral order on Earth. In the prophets, cosmic disturbances—like the sun darkening or stars falling—frequently symbolize divine judgment against systemic evil (Joel 2:30-31; Isaiah 13:10). While these texts use apocalyptic language, they highlight a profound relationship: the physical creation, which silently declares God's glory, also reflects His moral character.

Thus, when believers look to the heavens and marvel at the Creator's precision, they are also called to align themselves with the Creator's moral will. The logic is simple yet profound: if the cosmos is so carefully ordered that planets and stars move according to divinely set laws, then human society should likewise reflect a sense of moral harmony. That moral harmony, of course, has been disrupted by sin (Romans 8:22), leading to a creation that "groans" for renewal. Nonetheless, the consistent biblical refrain is that God's glory, declared by the heavens, also beckons humanity toward righteousness and love.

In a sense, the invitation to join the cosmic praise of God is also a summons to integrity. We are to be consistent with the divine imprint visible in nature—an imprint of both splendor and purposeful order. This moral dimension of cosmic order calls Christians not only to wonder and worship but also to practical obedience, ensuring that our actions on Earth resonate with the divine harmony that extends throughout the heavens.

Conclusion

In conclusion, **The Heavens Declare the Glory of God** is not a mere statement of poetic sentiment; it is a deep theological conviction that permeates the biblical narrative. Psalm 19 sets the tone by highlighting the universe as a universal proclamation of God's greatness, a message accessible to all people regardless of language or culture. Isaiah and Revelation expand this vision by placing cosmic imagery in the context of God's sovereign rule, moral governance, and redemptive plan for all of creation.

Against this backdrop, the question "Are we alone in this universe?" takes on a fresh dimension. If the heavens truly declare God's glory, then any discovery of extraterrestrial life would neither diminish God's majesty nor undermine the uniqueness of human existence. Rather, it would be another facet of a cosmos that already testifies to the richness of God's creative power. Whether or not we ever find such life, the conviction remains that the cosmos—brimming with galaxies, quasars, black holes, and untold wonders—proclaims the creativity and sovereignty of the One who spoke it into being.

For believers, the heavens are not an impersonal realm but the visible (and ever-more discoverable) handiwork of a God worthy of worship. This realization can transform how we approach science, art, and even daily life. Studying the cosmos can become an act of doxology, a way of echoing the silent praise of the stars. Appreciating the cosmic intricacies can lead to moral reflection on our responsibilities as stewards of Earth. Marveling at the possibility of other worlds can deepen humility and enlarge our perspective on the scope of God's love.

Chapter 3: Historical Christian Perspectives on Extraterrestrial Life

The question of life beyond Earth did not originate in the age of modern astronomy or science fiction. Early Christian authors and theologians, living in culturally diverse environments spanning the Roman Empire and beyond, sometimes touched on the nature of the cosmos in ways that might surprise contemporary readers. Whether intentionally or inadvertently, their musings laid the groundwork for later speculations and debates on extraterrestrial life.

In the medieval period, especially under the influence of Scholasticism, the idea that God's creation could encompass multiple forms of life, including angelic and perhaps even other physical beings, gained traction in some philosophical circles. Medieval theologians debated the structure of the universe, the nature of creation, and the possibility of multiple inhabited worlds —though they did so within strict doctrinal boundaries.

Fast-forward to the 19th and 20th centuries, and we encounter a broader range of Christian voices responding to the burgeoning field of astronomy and the cultural shifts wrought by industrialization and globalization. From novelists who wove theological themes into cosmic storylines to denominational statements addressing the scientific breakthroughs of their day, Christians increasingly encountered a reality in which multiple worlds, or at least the potential for multiple worlds, was becoming scientifically credible.

Throughout these eras, the fundamental tension has often remained the same: Does the Bible—or the wider Christian tradition—allow for life elsewhere, or does it situate humanity uniquely at the center of God's salvific plan? While conclusive answers remain elusive, historical Christian perspectives offer a rich tapestry of viewpoints, each shaped by its particular cultural, theological, and scientific context.

3.1. Early Church Speculations

3.1.1 Church Fathers and Cosmic Wonder

Beginnings of Cosmic Reflection

During the first few centuries of the Christian era, believers found themselves in a Greco-Roman cultural milieu where various philosophical schools had long debated the structure of reality. Thinkers like Plato and Aristotle had posited distinct cosmologies—some seeing Earth as unique, others allowing for multiple worlds in an infinite cosmos. Early Church Fathers did not always explicitly tackle the question of extraterrestrial life, but they inherited and sometimes reworked these philosophical frameworks to fit emerging Christian doctrine.

While overt speculation about alien life is sparse in surviving patristic writings, some Fathers invoked vast cosmic imagery to underscore God's omnipotence and creativity. For example, in his commentary on Genesis, Origen (c. 184–c. 253) often emphasized God's boundless power to create countless beings, both visible and invisible. Although he focused primarily on spiritual realms and the pre-existence of souls— a controversial view in later orthodox theology—Origen's readiness to conceive of innumerable worlds underscores an openness to cosmic diversity. He argued that if God is infinite, then the scope of creation might also be unfathomably large, with God potentially creating multiple orders of rational beings. These views, while not systematized into a formal doctrine of extraterrestrial life, hinted that the cosmos could be more populous than Earth alone.

Tensions with Gnosticism and Other Heresies

As Christian thinkers confronted groups like the Gnostics—who proposed intricate cosmologies involving various layers of divine and semi-divine entities—they sought to preserve core Christian affirmations: God's oneness, the created goodness of the material world, and the uniqueness of Christ's Incarnation. This made the early Church somewhat cautious about entertaining unrestrained speculation on multiple worlds or advanced beings beyond Earth, lest it blur the boundaries of orthodox teaching.

For instance, Tertullian (c. 155–c. 220) vigorously defended Christianity against Gnostic ideas that portrayed the physical cosmos as corrupt or the product of inferior deities. While Tertullian's writings often focused on moral and ecclesial issues, his broader argument was that the tangible, created world is fundamentally good because it comes from the one Creator God. Within this framework, if other inhabited realms did exist, they too would be under God's sovereign domain and shaped by divine goodness (cf. Genesis 1:31).

Augustine of Hippo (354–430), a towering figure in early Christian theology, touched on cosmological questions more explicitly. Though much of his writing pertains to Earth-centered concerns—original sin, grace, the City of God—he also recognized that Scripture's language about "heavens" might encompass vast realities not fully grasped by human observers. In *The City of God*, Augustine defends the unity of creation against Manichaean claims of an evil material world. While he does not speak directly of extraterrestrial life, he does stress that God's creative power extends indefinitely. One can infer that he would not have categorically dismissed the idea of other worlds; rather, he would have insisted that any such worlds remain subordinate to God's cosmic plan, centered on Christ (cf. Colossians 1:16-17).

Biblical References and Interpretations

In the early Church era, references to verses like John 14:2 ("In my Father's house are many rooms") sometimes appeared in homilies discussing the expansiveness of God's provision. While these passages more directly address spiritual abodes in heaven, some thinkers entertained broader applications. Certain theologians suggested these "rooms" could represent different realms of creation—not necessarily alien planets as we conceive of them today, but possibly indicating that God's household extends far beyond a single terrestrial sphere.

Equally pertinent was 1 Corinthians 4:9, which speaks of how the apostles were displayed as a spectacle "to the whole universe, to angels as well as to human beings." Patristic exegesis often focused on angels, but the underlying notion that the cosmos is an audience to earthly events introduced the possibility that other rational observers—beyond angelic hosts—might exist. Though not a mainstream patristic view, it demonstrates that the biblical text, even in the earliest centuries, could spark imaginative speculation regarding God's cosmic family.

3.1.2 Medieval Scholastics and the Hierarchy of Creation

Shifts in Cosmological Understanding

Moving into the medieval period (roughly the 5th to the 15th centuries), Christian perspectives on the cosmos were influenced by the Aristotelian-Ptolemaic model, which placed Earth at the center of concentric celestial spheres. This geocentric view was not inherently anti-extraterrestrial, but it often implied a hierarchical order in which earthly life held a unique, if not exclusive, position in the physical realm.

Nonetheless, medieval thought—especially under the Scholastics—was not static. Figures like Thomas Aquinas

(1225–1274) grappled with reconciling Aristotelian philosophy with Christian doctrine. While Aquinas did not explicitly teach that there are inhabited worlds beyond Earth, his theology allowed for the possibility of a multiplicity of creations, visible and invisible. Aquinas's extensive writings on angels, for example, highlight the existence of intelligent beings distinct from humans, indicating that God's creative repertoire is not limited to one type of rational creature.

One crucial tenet for medieval theologians was the notion of *creatio ex nihilo* ("creation out of nothing"), which underscored divine sovereignty over all that exists. This principle opened the door, at least theoretically, for God to create manifold worlds if He so desired. To say that Earth was the only realm with life was not necessarily guaranteed by Scripture or doctrine. Yet, the lack of observational evidence and the philosophical frameworks of the time often kept such speculation at bay.

The Great Chain of Being

Medieval Christian cosmology often embraced the concept of the "Great Chain of Being," a hierarchical structure stretching from inanimate matter at the bottom to God at the top, with angels, humans, animals, and plants arranged in between. Each level had its assigned place, reflecting divine order. This hierarchy accommodated an incredible variety of creatures, from earthly and material to spiritual and celestial.

While the Great Chain of Being did not automatically include "extraterrestrials" in the modern sense, it set a precedent for thinking that there could be intermediate or additional forms of life not explicitly described in Scripture. Angels and demons, for instance, represented categories of intelligent beings different from humanity yet integral to the Christian understanding of reality (cf. Hebrews 1:14). If cosmic diversity was an expression of God's creative exuberance, then the idea that the chain might have "links" we had not yet discovered was not entirely foreign to the scholastic imagination.

However, medieval theologians were bound by orthodox interpretations of passages that placed humanity in a central narrative role—especially those detailing the Incarnation and Resurrection of Jesus. Consequently, any speculation about other life forms had to respect the unique role of Christ's redeeming work on Earth. This tension set the stage for future debates: if other rational beings existed, did they require redemption, and if so, how did Christ's once-for-all sacrifice apply to them? Though medieval discussions rarely addressed this point directly, the seeds of inquiry were planted.

Biblical Echoes in Medieval Thought

While medieval theology heavily relied on reason and philosophical categories, Scripture remained paramount. Passages like Job 38, where God challenges Job to consider the extent of creation, and Psalm 148, which calls upon heavenly and earthly realms alike to praise the Lord, were frequently cited to underscore that creation's variety testifies to God's glory. Medieval commentators often emphasized that the universe, in all its layers, is orchestrated for divine purposes.

Some scholars saw John 1:3 ("All things were made through him, and without him was not any thing made that was made") as a basis for cosmic unity—everything that exists has a share in the creative Word of God. Though the details about inhabited worlds were not fleshed out, the verse implied that if such worlds exist, they, too, were fashioned through the Logos. This line of reasoning would later shape modern theological discourse, as Christians wrestled with the implications of an expanding universe.

3.2. Modern Theological Discourse

3.2.1 19th and 20th-Century Voices

The Impact of Scientific Developments

The advent of telescopes and the rise of modern astronomy in the 17th and 18th centuries laid the groundwork for the 19th and 20th centuries, when the universe appeared vastly larger and more complex than previously imagined. The Copernican Revolution had already dethroned Earth from the cosmic center, and subsequent observations by astronomers like William Herschel revealed that our solar system is but one of countless star systems within a massive galaxy. Later, Edwin Hubble's findings in the early 20th century showed that the Milky Way is only one of many galaxies scattered across an immense cosmos.

Christians from various denominational backgrounds reacted to these discoveries in diverse ways. Some voiced concern that Earth's seemingly diminished physical status in the universe might undermine the special role of humanity in salvation history. Others embraced the new data as evidence of God's boundless creative power, seeing in a populated cosmos merely another chapter in the ongoing revelation of divine majesty.

One influential stream of Christian thought posited that if the cosmos is so vast, it might be teeming with life. The Scottish theologian Thomas Chalmers (1780–1847) famously argued that the Incarnation of Christ on Earth did not necessarily preclude other inhabited worlds. Citing biblical passages that underscore God's dominion over all things (Psalm 103:19; Ephesians 1:20-21), Chalmers suggested that God's relationship with the human race could be unique in some respects while leaving open the possibility that other races exist under different divine arrangements.

Christian Novelists and Cultural Shifts

By the late 19th century, science fiction as a literary genre began to emerge, sometimes infused with religious or theological themes. Authors like Jules Verne and H.G. Wells, though not strictly writing from Christian perspectives, sparked public fascination with planetary travel and alien worlds. Meanwhile, Christian authors such as George MacDonald (1824–1905) and later C.S. Lewis (1898–1963) created imaginative narratives that included otherworldly beings and cosmic journeys, weaving in Christian allegory or moral reflections.

MacDonald, a Scottish minister, used fantasy and fairy-tale motifs to engage theological ideas, occasionally hinting at the immensity of creation. C.S. Lewis went further in his *Space Trilogy* (*Out of the Silent Planet, Perelandra, That Hideous Strength*), envisioning inhabited planets—Malacandra (Mars) and Perelandra (Venus)—where unfallen races existed, each under the overarching rule of Maleldil (a Christ-like figure). Though clearly fictional, Lewis's works open a window into mid-20th-century Christian imagination regarding extraterrestrial life. He proposed that God's cosmic plan could embrace multiple species, each with its own journey under the same Creator.

Even Lewis's fictional approach provoked theological reflection. If sin had corrupted only Earth (the "Silent Planet"), what would that imply about the universal reach of the Incarnation? Could humans be quarantined in a fallen state, while other races remain in harmony with God? These questions tapped into a vein of thought that had been dormant since the medieval period, reignited now by the plausibility of an immense, life-friendly universe.

Vatican Engagement and Broader Conversations

In the Roman Catholic Church, the Vatican's historical involvement with astronomy (e.g., the Vatican Observatory) showcased a willingness to dialogue between faith and science. By the early 20th century, some Catholic theologians and astronomers publicly entertained the idea that discovering extraterrestrial life would not necessarily contradict Christian doctrine. The Jesuit astronomer Angelo Secchi (1818–1878) had earlier advocated for close cooperation between science and religion, remarking that the pursuit of astronomical knowledge often deepens spiritual awe rather than diminishing it.

Decades later, astronomers like Guy Consolmagno, also a Jesuit and director of the Vatican Observatory, would echo such sentiments in public statements. Consolmagno has stated that believing in a universe teeming with life need not conflict with core Christian beliefs, including the uniqueness of Christ's Incarnation. Instead, he argues, it could reveal the depth of God's creative freedom. While official dogmatic pronouncements on aliens remain absent, the Vatican's engagement with astronomy illustrates a continuity of thought dating back to medieval scholasticism: God's sovereignty is not constrained by human assumptions about Earth's privileged place.

Protestant denominations, too, saw robust debate. Liberal Protestant theologians in the 19th century often embraced the concept of cosmic pluralism, linking it to a progressive vision of God's evolving creation. Conservative Protestants varied in their responses—some adopting more literal readings of Scripture that favored Earth-centric creation, while others allowed that God's creative liberty could include beings elsewhere. Through sermons, commentaries, and theological journals, the conversation gradually expanded, reflecting growing awareness of cosmic immensity.

3.2.2 Denominational Approaches

Evangelical Perspectives

Within the broad umbrella of evangelical Christianity, perspectives on extraterrestrial life have ranged widely. Some evangelicals hold that Earth is the singular cradle of God's image-bearing creatures, citing passages like Romans 8:19-22, where all of creation "waits in eager expectation" for human redemption, presumably centering cosmic significance on humanity's fall and salvation. For these believers, the Incarnation of Christ on Earth places humanity at a unique spiritual apex, leaving little room for speculations about alien civilizations.

Yet other evangelical voices argue that God's boundless grace could encompass multiple worlds, each with its own story. They stress the distinction between biblical authority and the realm of scientific inquiry, suggesting that Scripture need not be read as prohibiting extraterrestrial life. This group often references John 10:16 ("I have other sheep that are not of this fold") as a metaphorical nod—while likely referring to Gentile inclusion in the early Church, the phrase resonates with the possibility that God might have "other flocks" across the cosmos.

Mainline Protestant Perspectives

Mainline Protestant traditions, such as Anglicanism, Lutheranism, and certain Reformed churches, generally emphasize the compatibility of faith and scientific exploration. Historically, these denominations have been open to discussing the broader universe in light of biblical faith. Official statements on alien life remain uncommon, but church leaders within these traditions often encourage scientific inquiry, affirming that a larger cosmos filled with diverse life forms would magnify, rather than challenge, God's glory.

In the Anglican tradition, for instance, theologians have sometimes referenced the "principle of plenitude," the idea that a perfect Creator might bring forth every conceivable form of existence—an argument dating back to medieval theology. This principle does not guarantee aliens exist, but it refuses to close the door on their possibility. Within Lutheran circles, the emphasis on salvation by grace alone might prompt speculation about how such grace would manifest if other intelligent beings exist—a question that usually ends with humility before the mystery of God's redemptive plan. Reformed thought, shaped by ideas of God's sovereignty, could similarly allow that God's purposes extend well beyond the confines of Earth's story.

Roman Catholic and Orthodox Views

As mentioned, the Roman Catholic Church does not have a dogmatic statement on extraterrestrial life. Nevertheless, Catholic theology, with its robust emphasis on natural law and the goodness of creation, has room to accommodate cosmic diversity. Some Catholic theologians speculate that if rational aliens exist, they might also share in the fundamental call to know and love God—a call that, in Christian belief, finds its fullness in Christ's self-revelation. Whether that self-revelation would take the same form (the Incarnation on Earth) or another mode remains an open theological question.

In Eastern Orthodoxy, cosmic wonder often intersects with a strong emphasis on the mystical encounter with God. Writers in the Orthodox tradition sometimes point to the Transfiguration of Christ (Matthew 17:1-9) as a glimpse of cosmic renewal, a foretaste of divine light permeating all creation. While explicit discussions of ET life are less common in Orthodox texts, the theology of deification (theosis) sees all creation as destined for union with God's uncreated energies. In principle, that perspective could include any and all sentient beings within the cosmos.

Ecumenical Conversations

In the 20th century, ecumenical movements brought different Christian traditions into dialogue, sometimes addressing questions of science and faith in official councils or statements. While few ecumenical documents directly tackled extraterrestrial life, many affirmed the broader idea that scientific inquiry into the universe should be welcomed as part of humanity's God-given curiosity and stewardship mandate (cf. Genesis 2:15). These statements, though often general, imply that discovering alien civilizations, if it ever happened, would not necessarily undermine Christian unity but rather call for renewed theological reflection across denominational lines.

From these varied denominational responses emerges a landscape in which some Christians hold firmly to Earth's privileged spiritual role, while others eagerly embrace the possibility that God's plan for creation includes other rational beings. In all cases, the core affirmations of the faith—God's sovereignty, Christ's redemptive action, and the call to love God and neighbor—remain central. The question of "Are we alone?" becomes an avenue for deeper exploration of these mysteries rather than a threat to established doctrine.

Conclusion

Across nearly two millennia of Christian history, the prospect of extraterrestrial life has quietly hovered at the edges of theological inquiry, sometimes taking center stage during moments of significant scientific or philosophical change. The early Church Fathers, grappling with Greco-Roman cosmologies and heretical views, laid a groundwork of openness—however understated—to a vast creation that could, in principle, include a wide range of beings. In the medieval period, Scholastics wrestled with philosophical frameworks that placed Earth in a geocentric cosmos yet simultaneously acknowledged the multiplicity of God's creative acts. This tension foreshadowed the more explicit debates that would unfold in modern times.

The 19th and 20th centuries brought an explosion of astronomical discoveries, coupled with cultural phenomena such as science fiction, both of which spurred Christians to revisit biblical teachings in a new cosmic light. The result was—and continues to be—a spectrum of theological opinions. Some remain grounded in a view that elevates Earth and humanity as uniquely central to God's salvific narrative, while others see in the vastness of space an opportunity to celebrate the possibility of life forms unknown to us, all under the umbrella of God's universal grace. Denominations differ not so much on whether God *could* have created other beings, but on how such a reality would intersect with doctrines of the Incarnation, sin, and redemption.

If there is a unifying thread in these historical perspectives, it may be the recognition that Christian theology has always adapted and responded to new knowledge about the natural world. Whether that knowledge came from pagan philosophers in the early centuries, medieval Scholastics in dialogue with Aristotle, or modern astronomers and novelists reimagining the cosmos, the core question remained: How does this knowledge illuminate, deepen, or challenge our understanding of God's creative power and saving love?

In concluding this chapter, we observe that historical Christian thought on extraterrestrial life offers no single, conclusive answer—but it does provide a scripture of creative, often daring, attempts to reconcile the immensity of God's universe with the specifics of Christian doctrine. The centuries-long conversation shows that whenever new vistas open up in our understanding of creation, Christians from every tradition have found ways to see those vistas as further reason to praise the Creator. The story, of course, is not finished. As new discoveries emerge, this deep-rooted tradition of inquiry and reverent wonder will undoubtedly continue, shaping future Christian perspectives on whether—and how—we might share the cosmos with others.

Chapter 3: Historical Christian Perspectives on Extraterrestrial Life

The question of life beyond Earth did not originate in the age of modern astronomy or science fiction. Early Christian authors and theologians, living in culturally diverse environments spanning the Roman Empire and beyond, sometimes touched on the nature of the cosmos in ways that might surprise contemporary readers. Whether intentionally or inadvertently, their musings laid the groundwork for later speculations and debates on extraterrestrial life.

In the medieval period, especially under the influence of Scholasticism, the idea that God's creation could encompass multiple forms of life, including angelic and perhaps even other physical beings, gained traction in some philosophical circles. Medieval theologians debated the structure of the universe, the nature of creation, and the possibility of multiple inhabited worlds—though they did so within strict doctrinal boundaries.

Fast-forward to the 19th and 20th centuries, and we encounter a broader range of Christian voices responding to the burgeoning field of astronomy and the cultural shifts wrought by industrialization and globalization. From novelists who wove theological themes into cosmic storylines to denominational statements addressing the scientific breakthroughs of their day, Christians increasingly encountered a reality in which multiple worlds, or at least the potential for multiple worlds, was becoming scientifically credible.

Throughout these eras, the fundamental tension has often remained the same: Does the Bible—or the wider Christian tradition—allow for life elsewhere, or does it situate humanity uniquely at the center of God's salvific plan? While conclusive answers remain elusive, historical Christian perspectives offer a rich tapestry of viewpoints, each shaped by its particular cultural, theological, and scientific context.

3.1. Early Church Speculations

3.1.1 Church Fathers and Cosmic Wonder

Beginnings of Cosmic Reflection

During the first few centuries of the Christian era, believers found themselves in a Greco-Roman cultural milieu where various philosophical schools had long debated the structure of reality. Thinkers like Plato and Aristotle had posited distinct cosmologies—some seeing Earth as unique, others allowing for multiple worlds in an infinite cosmos. Early Church Fathers did not always explicitly tackle the question of extraterrestrial life, but they inherited and sometimes reworked these philosophical frameworks to fit emerging Christian doctrine.

While overt speculation about alien life is sparse in surviving patristic writings, some Fathers invoked vast cosmic imagery to underscore God's omnipotence and creativity. For example, in his commentary on Genesis, Origen (c. 184–c. 253) often emphasized God's boundless power to create countless beings, both visible and invisible. Although he focused primarily on spiritual realms and the pre-existence of souls— a controversial view in later orthodox theology—Origen's readiness to conceive of innumerable worlds underscores an openness to cosmic diversity. He argued that if God is infinite, then the scope of creation might also be unfathomably large, with God potentially creating multiple orders of rational beings. These views, while not systematized into a formal doctrine of extraterrestrial life, hinted that the cosmos could be more populous than Earth alone.

Tensions with Gnosticism and Other Heresies

As Christian thinkers confronted groups like the Gnostics— who proposed intricate cosmologies involving various layers of divine and semi-divine entities—they sought to preserve core Christian affirmations: God's oneness, the created goodness of the material world, and the uniqueness of Christ's Incarnation. This made the early Church somewhat cautious about entertaining unrestrained speculation on multiple worlds or advanced beings beyond Earth, lest it blur the boundaries of orthodox teaching.

For instance, Tertullian (c. 155–c. 220) vigorously defended Christianity against Gnostic ideas that portrayed the physical cosmos as corrupt or the product of inferior deities. While Tertullian's writings often focused on moral and ecclesial issues, his broader argument was that the tangible, created world is fundamentally good because it comes from the one Creator God. Within this framework, if other inhabited realms did exist, they too would be under God's sovereign domain and shaped by divine goodness (cf. Genesis 1:31).

Augustine of Hippo (354–430), a towering figure in early Christian theology, touched on cosmological questions more explicitly. Though much of his writing pertains to Earth-centered concerns—original sin, grace, the City of God—he also recognized that Scripture's language about "heavens" might encompass vast realities not fully grasped by human observers. In *The City of God*, Augustine defends the unity of creation against Manichaean claims of an evil material world. While he does not speak directly of extraterrestrial life, he does stress that God's creative power extends indefinitely. One can infer that he would not have categorically dismissed the idea of other worlds; rather, he would have insisted that any such worlds remain subordinate to God's cosmic plan, centered on Christ (cf. Colossians 1:16-17).

Biblical References and Interpretations

In the early Church era, references to verses like John 14:2 ("In my Father's house are many rooms") sometimes appeared in homilies discussing the expansiveness of God's provision. While these passages more directly address spiritual abodes in heaven, some thinkers entertained broader applications. Certain theologians suggested these "rooms" could represent different realms of creation—not necessarily alien planets as we conceive of them today, but possibly indicating that God's household extends far beyond a single terrestrial sphere.

Equally pertinent was 1 Corinthians 4:9, which speaks of how the apostles were displayed as a spectacle "to the whole universe, to angels as well as to human beings." Patristic exegesis often focused on angels, but the underlying notion that the cosmos is an audience to earthly events introduced the possibility that other rational observers—beyond angelic hosts—might exist. Though not a mainstream patristic view, it demonstrates that the biblical text, even in the earliest centuries, could spark imaginative speculation regarding God's cosmic family.

3.1.2 Medieval Scholastics and the Hierarchy of Creation

Shifts in Cosmological Understanding

Moving into the medieval period (roughly the 5th to the 15th centuries), Christian perspectives on the cosmos were influenced by the Aristotelian-Ptolemaic model, which placed Earth at the center of concentric celestial spheres. This geocentric view was not inherently anti-extraterrestrial, but it often implied a hierarchical order in which earthly life held a unique, if not exclusive, position in the physical realm.

Nonetheless, medieval thought—especially under the Scholastics—was not static. Figures like Thomas Aquinas

(1225–1274) grappled with reconciling Aristotelian philosophy with Christian doctrine. While Aquinas did not explicitly teach that there are inhabited worlds beyond Earth, his theology allowed for the possibility of a multiplicity of creations, visible and invisible. Aquinas's extensive writings on angels, for example, highlight the existence of intelligent beings distinct from humans, indicating that God's creative repertoire is not limited to one type of rational creature.

One crucial tenet for medieval theologians was the notion of *creatio ex nihilo* ("creation out of nothing"), which underscored divine sovereignty over all that exists. This principle opened the door, at least theoretically, for God to create manifold worlds if He so desired. To say that Earth was the only realm with life was not necessarily guaranteed by Scripture or doctrine. Yet, the lack of observational evidence and the philosophical frameworks of the time often kept such speculation at bay.

The Great Chain of Being

Medieval Christian cosmology often embraced the concept of the "Great Chain of Being," a hierarchical structure stretching from inanimate matter at the bottom to God at the top, with angels, humans, animals, and plants arranged in between. Each level had its assigned place, reflecting divine order. This hierarchy accommodated an incredible variety of creatures, from earthly and material to spiritual and celestial.

While the Great Chain of Being did not automatically include "extraterrestrials" in the modern sense, it set a precedent for thinking that there could be intermediate or additional forms of life not explicitly described in Scripture. Angels and demons, for instance, represented categories of intelligent beings different from humanity yet integral to the Christian understanding of reality (cf. Hebrews 1:14). If cosmic diversity was an expression of God's creative exuberance, then the idea that the chain might have "links" we had not yet discovered was not entirely foreign to the scholastic imagination.

However, medieval theologians were bound by orthodox interpretations of passages that placed humanity in a central narrative role—especially those detailing the Incarnation and Resurrection of Jesus. Consequently, any speculation about other life forms had to respect the unique role of Christ's redeeming work on Earth. This tension set the stage for future debates: if other rational beings existed, did they require redemption, and if so, how did Christ's once-for-all sacrifice apply to them? Though medieval discussions rarely addressed this point directly, the seeds of inquiry were planted.

Biblical Echoes in Medieval Thought

While medieval theology heavily relied on reason and philosophical categories, Scripture remained paramount. Passages like Job 38, where God challenges Job to consider the extent of creation, and Psalm 148, which calls upon heavenly and earthly realms alike to praise the Lord, were frequently cited to underscore that creation's variety testifies to God's glory. Medieval commentators often emphasized that the universe, in all its layers, is orchestrated for divine purposes.

Some scholars saw John 1:3 ("All things were made through him, and without him was not any thing made that was made") as a basis for cosmic unity—everything that exists has a share in the creative Word of God. Though the details about inhabited worlds were not fleshed out, the verse implied that if such worlds exist, they, too, were fashioned through the Logos. This line of reasoning would later shape modern theological discourse, as Christians wrestled with the implications of an expanding universe.

3.2. Modern Theological Discourse

3.2.1 19th and 20th-Century Voices

The Impact of Scientific Developments

The advent of telescopes and the rise of modern astronomy in the 17th and 18th centuries laid the groundwork for the 19th and 20th centuries, when the universe appeared vastly larger and more complex than previously imagined. The Copernican Revolution had already dethroned Earth from the cosmic center, and subsequent observations by astronomers like William Herschel revealed that our solar system is but one of countless star systems within a massive galaxy. Later, Edwin Hubble's findings in the early 20th century showed that the Milky Way is only one of many galaxies scattered across an immense cosmos.

Christians from various denominational backgrounds reacted to these discoveries in diverse ways. Some voiced concern that Earth's seemingly diminished physical status in the universe might undermine the special role of humanity in salvation history. Others embraced the new data as evidence of God's boundless creative power, seeing in a populated cosmos merely another chapter in the ongoing revelation of divine majesty.

One influential stream of Christian thought posited that if the cosmos is so vast, it might be teeming with life. The Scottish theologian Thomas Chalmers (1780–1847) famously argued that the Incarnation of Christ on Earth did not necessarily preclude other inhabited worlds. Citing biblical passages that underscore God's dominion over all things (Psalm 103:19; Ephesians 1:20-21), Chalmers suggested that God's relationship with the human race could be unique in some respects while leaving open the possibility that other races exist under different divine arrangements.

Christian Novelists and Cultural Shifts

By the late 19th century, science fiction as a literary genre began to emerge, sometimes infused with religious or theological themes. Authors like Jules Verne and H.G. Wells, though not strictly writing from Christian perspectives, sparked public fascination with planetary travel and alien worlds. Meanwhile, Christian authors such as George MacDonald (1824–1905) and later C.S. Lewis (1898–1963) created imaginative narratives that included otherworldly beings and cosmic journeys, weaving in Christian allegory or moral reflections.

MacDonald, a Scottish minister, used fantasy and fairy-tale motifs to engage theological ideas, occasionally hinting at the immensity of creation. C.S. Lewis went further in his *Space Trilogy* (*Out of the Silent Planet*, *Perelandra*, *That Hideous Strength*), envisioning inhabited planets—Malacandra (Mars) and Perelandra (Venus)—where unfallen races existed, each under the overarching rule of Maleldil (a Christ-like figure). Though clearly fictional, Lewis's works open a window into mid-20th-century Christian imagination regarding extraterrestrial life. He proposed that God's cosmic plan could embrace multiple species, each with its own journey under the same Creator.

Even Lewis's fictional approach provoked theological reflection. If sin had corrupted only Earth (the "Silent Planet"), what would that imply about the universal reach of the Incarnation? Could humans be quarantined in a fallen state, while other races remain in harmony with God? These questions tapped into a vein of thought that had been dormant since the medieval period, reignited now by the plausibility of an immense, life-friendly universe.

Vatican Engagement and Broader Conversations

In the Roman Catholic Church, the Vatican's historical involvement with astronomy (e.g., the Vatican Observatory) showcased a willingness to dialogue between faith and science. By the early 20th century, some Catholic theologians and astronomers publicly entertained the idea that discovering extraterrestrial life would not necessarily contradict Christian doctrine. The Jesuit astronomer Angelo Secchi (1818–1878) had earlier advocated for close cooperation between science and religion, remarking that the pursuit of astronomical knowledge often deepens spiritual awe rather than diminishing it.

Decades later, astronomers like Guy Consolmagno, also a Jesuit and director of the Vatican Observatory, would echo such sentiments in public statements. Consolmagno has stated that believing in a universe teeming with life need not conflict with core Christian beliefs, including the uniqueness of Christ's Incarnation. Instead, he argues, it could reveal the depth of God's creative freedom. While official dogmatic pronouncements on aliens remain absent, the Vatican's engagement with astronomy illustrates a continuity of thought dating back to medieval scholasticism: God's sovereignty is not constrained by human assumptions about Earth's privileged place.

Protestant denominations, too, saw robust debate. Liberal Protestant theologians in the 19th century often embraced the concept of cosmic pluralism, linking it to a progressive vision of God's evolving creation. Conservative Protestants varied in their responses—some adopting more literal readings of Scripture that favored Earth-centric creation, while others allowed that God's creative liberty could include beings elsewhere. Through sermons, commentaries, and theological journals, the conversation gradually expanded, reflecting growing awareness of cosmic immensity.

3.2.2 Denominational Approaches

Evangelical Perspectives

Within the broad umbrella of evangelical Christianity, perspectives on extraterrestrial life have ranged widely. Some evangelicals hold that Earth is the singular cradle of God's image-bearing creatures, citing passages like Romans 8:19-22, where all of creation "waits in eager expectation" for human redemption, presumably centering cosmic significance on humanity's fall and salvation. For these believers, the Incarnation of Christ on Earth places humanity at a unique spiritual apex, leaving little room for speculations about alien civilizations.

Yet other evangelical voices argue that God's boundless grace could encompass multiple worlds, each with its own story. They stress the distinction between biblical authority and the realm of scientific inquiry, suggesting that Scripture need not be read as prohibiting extraterrestrial life. This group often references John 10:16 ("I have other sheep that are not of this fold") as a metaphorical nod—while likely referring to Gentile inclusion in the early Church, the phrase resonates with the possibility that God might have "other flocks" across the cosmos.

Mainline Protestant Perspectives

Mainline Protestant traditions, such as Anglicanism, Lutheranism, and certain Reformed churches, generally emphasize the compatibility of faith and scientific exploration. Historically, these denominations have been open to discussing the broader universe in light of biblical faith. Official statements on alien life remain uncommon, but church leaders within these traditions often encourage scientific inquiry, affirming that a larger cosmos filled with diverse life forms would magnify, rather than challenge, God's glory.

In the Anglican tradition, for instance, theologians have sometimes referenced the "principle of plenitude," the idea that a perfect Creator might bring forth every conceivable form of existence—an argument dating back to medieval theology. This principle does not guarantee aliens exist, but it refuses to close the door on their possibility. Within Lutheran circles, the emphasis on salvation by grace alone might prompt speculation about how such grace would manifest if other intelligent beings exist—a question that usually ends with humility before the mystery of God's redemptive plan. Reformed thought, shaped by ideas of God's sovereignty, could similarly allow that God's purposes extend well beyond the confines of Earth's story.

Roman Catholic and Orthodox Views

As mentioned, the Roman Catholic Church does not have a dogmatic statement on extraterrestrial life. Nevertheless, Catholic theology, with its robust emphasis on natural law and the goodness of creation, has room to accommodate cosmic diversity. Some Catholic theologians speculate that if rational aliens exist, they might also share in the fundamental call to know and love God—a call that, in Christian belief, finds its fullness in Christ's self-revelation. Whether that self-revelation would take the same form (the Incarnation on Earth) or another mode remains an open theological question.

In Eastern Orthodoxy, cosmic wonder often intersects with a strong emphasis on the mystical encounter with God. Writers in the Orthodox tradition sometimes point to the Transfiguration of Christ (Matthew 17:1-9) as a glimpse of cosmic renewal, a foretaste of divine light permeating all creation. While explicit discussions of ET life are less common in Orthodox texts, the theology of deification (theosis) sees all creation as destined for union with God's uncreated energies. In principle, that perspective could include any and all sentient beings within the cosmos.

Ecumenical Conversations

In the 20th century, ecumenical movements brought different Christian traditions into dialogue, sometimes addressing questions of science and faith in official councils or statements. While few ecumenical documents directly tackled extraterrestrial life, many affirmed the broader idea that scientific inquiry into the universe should be welcomed as part of humanity's God-given curiosity and stewardship mandate (cf. Genesis 2:15). These statements, though often general, imply that discovering alien civilizations, if it ever happened, would not necessarily undermine Christian unity but rather call for renewed theological reflection across denominational lines.

From these varied denominational responses emerges a landscape in which some Christians hold firmly to Earth's privileged spiritual role, while others eagerly embrace the possibility that God's plan for creation includes other rational beings. In all cases, the core affirmations of the faith—God's sovereignty, Christ's redemptive action, and the call to love God and neighbor—remain central. The question of "Are we alone?" becomes an avenue for deeper exploration of these mysteries rather than a threat to established doctrine.

Conclusion

Across nearly two millennia of Christian history, the prospect of extraterrestrial life has quietly hovered at the edges of theological inquiry, sometimes taking center stage during moments of significant scientific or philosophical change. The early Church Fathers, grappling with Greco-Roman cosmologies and heretical views, laid a groundwork of openness—however understated—to a vast creation that could, in principle, include a wide range of beings. In the medieval period, Scholastics wrestled with philosophical frameworks that placed Earth in a geocentric cosmos yet simultaneously acknowledged the multiplicity of God's creative acts. This tension foreshadowed the more explicit debates that would unfold in modern times.

The 19th and 20th centuries brought an explosion of astronomical discoveries, coupled with cultural phenomena such as science fiction, both of which spurred Christians to revisit biblical teachings in a new cosmic light. The result was—and continues to be—a spectrum of theological opinions. Some remain grounded in a view that elevates Earth and humanity as uniquely central to God's salvific narrative, while others see in the vastness of space an opportunity to celebrate the possibility of life forms unknown to us, all under the umbrella of God's universal grace. Denominations differ not so much on whether God *could* have created other beings, but on how such a reality would intersect with doctrines of the Incarnation, sin, and redemption.

If there is a unifying thread in these historical perspectives, it may be the recognition that Christian theology has always adapted and responded to new knowledge about the natural world. Whether that knowledge came from pagan philosophers in the early centuries, medieval Scholastics in dialogue with Aristotle, or modern astronomers and novelists reimagining the cosmos, the core question remained: How does this knowledge illuminate, deepen, or challenge our understanding of God's creative power and saving love?

In concluding this chapter, we observe that historical Christian thought on extraterrestrial life offers no single, conclusive answer—but it does provide a scripture of creative, often daring, attempts to reconcile the immensity of God's universe with the specifics of Christian doctrine. The centuries-long conversation shows that whenever new vistas open up in our understanding of creation, Christians from every tradition have found ways to see those vistas as further reason to praise the Creator. The story, of course, is not finished. As new discoveries emerge, this deep-rooted tradition of inquiry and reverent wonder will undoubtedly continue, shaping future Christian perspectives on whether—and how—we might share the cosmos with others.

Chapter 4: Astronomy and the Scope of the Universe

Modern astronomy represents one of humanity's most far-reaching intellectual endeavors. What began with simple naked-eye observations—recording lunar phases and the wandering paths of planets—has grown into a sophisticated science capable of detecting distant galaxies billions of light-years away. Alongside physics, chemistry, and other fields, astronomy has helped reveal that our Sun is only one star among countless others in the Milky Way, and our galaxy itself is but a speck among trillions in the observable universe.

While technology has revolutionized how and what we see, the philosophical and spiritual implications remain profound. The psalmist's declaration that God "determines the number of the stars; he gives to all of them their names" (Psalm 147:4) resonates anew in an age when new stars are cataloged daily. The cosmic scale invites humility and wonder, echoing Isaiah's challenge to "lift up your eyes on high and see: who created these?" (Isaiah 40:26). For people of faith, the unfolding story of astronomical discovery raises questions about God's relationship to a cosmos so immense that our home planet appears infinitesimal by comparison. And yet, from a biblical standpoint, God's care is never diminished by the universe's size.

4.1. Emerging Scientific Discoveries

4.1.1 From Galileo to Hubble

The Telescope's Transformative Power

Although ancient astronomers in Babylon, Egypt, China, and Greece laid foundational concepts for mapping the heavens, the modern era of astronomy is often traced to Galileo Galilei (1564–1642). Galileo's use of the telescope revolutionized how humans perceived the universe. Prior to him, celestial observations relied on the naked eye, which could see a few thousand stars at best and interpret planetary motion in only a rough sense. With the aid of a telescope—primitive by current standards but groundbreaking in its time—Galileo discovered Jupiter's four largest moons, observed the phases of Venus, and revealed innumerable new stars in the Milky Way.

Galileo's findings lent critical support to the heliocentric model advocated by Nicolaus Copernicus, dislodging Earth from its presumed central position in the cosmos. The controversy that ensued was not merely scientific but also theological, as many ecclesiastical authorities had long aligned with a geocentric view. Yet the deeper impact was existential: if Earth was not the fixed center, then the universe might be vastly larger than previously thought, with Earth occupying no special spatial location. Galileo's work thus catalyzed a new mindset—one in which humans could no longer assume that the cosmos existed solely for terrestrial drama. Although he did not directly propose extraterrestrial life, his observations expanded the conceptual space for that possibility.

Expanding Perspectives: Newton to Herschel

Following Galileo, Sir Isaac Newton (1642–1727) formulated his law of universal gravitation, revealing that the same physical principles govern both terrestrial and celestial motion.

This unity of natural law implied that the cosmos was not a patchwork of unrelated phenomena but a grand system held together by elegant, predictable principles. Though often taken for granted today, Newton's insights were revolutionary. If the laws of physics are universal, then stars, planets, and any potential life beyond Earth would obey the same cosmic "rules" we see in action locally.

During the 18th century, astronomers like William Herschel (1738–1822) and Caroline Herschel (1750–1848) carried astronomy further, systematically cataloging stars and nebulae. William Herschel discovered the planet Uranus in 1781—an event that expanded our solar system beyond the classical planets known to ancient civilizations. As he scanned the skies, Herschel speculated about life on other planets, including even the Sun, revealing a spirit of cosmic curiosity that dovetailed with a growing acceptance of pluralism (the idea of multiple inhabited worlds). Although we now know the Sun is not a habitable environment, Herschel's inquisitiveness exemplified a shifting perspective: more and more, the cosmic stage appeared too large and too varied to host only one form of advanced life.

The 19th Century: Charting the Heavens

By the 19th century, astronomy became increasingly systematic, aided by improved telescopes and photographic techniques. Observatories sprang up across Europe and the United States, each vying for deeper looks into celestial phenomena. The development of spectroscopy—where starlight is split into its component wavelengths—allowed astronomers to identify the chemical composition of stars. The realization that stars consist of elements common on Earth (primarily hydrogen and helium, along with smaller amounts of heavier elements) further underscored the cosmic principle of uniformity: we are, in the words of many modern scientists, "stardust." If Earth's elements exist universally, then the potential for life-sustaining chemistry might also exist elsewhere.

Biblical reflections during this period often referenced verses like Psalm 19:1 ("The heavens declare the glory of God") to affirm that new astronomical insights deepened, rather than threatened, Christian belief. The vast number of stars charted by 19th-century astronomers expanded the sense of awe, leading some theologians to suggest that the creation accounts in Scripture were never meant to provide a complete inventory of cosmic bodies but to point humanity toward worship of the One who fashioned them all.

Leap into the 20th Century: Relativity and the Expanding Universe

The dawn of the 20th century brought two monumental breakthroughs: Einstein's theory of relativity and Edwin Hubble's observations that the universe is expanding. Prior to Hubble, the prevailing view held that our galaxy, the Milky Way, encompassed most of the known cosmos. Yet when Hubble measured the distance to spiral "nebulae" like Andromeda, he demonstrated that these were entire galaxies beyond the Milky Way. The scale of reality thus mushroomed almost overnight. Hubble also discovered that galaxies are moving away from one another, implying that space itself is stretching—an observation that eventually led to the Big Bang theory.

These findings dramatically widened the canvas for speculation about extraterrestrial life. If galaxies number in the hundreds of billions, each containing hundreds of billions of stars, the total number of potential planetary systems is staggering. With so many possible homes for life, some scientists estimated that the cosmos might be filled with civilizations beyond counting. While direct confirmation remained elusive, the notion that the universe might harbor a multitude of life forms grew from fringe speculation to a topic of legitimate scientific inquiry.

Religious Reactions: Cautious Openness

Christian voices, for the most part, have responded to these astronomical milestones with a mixture of excitement and theological reflection. Even among more traditional churches, many have concluded that the newfound enormity of the universe magnifies, rather than negates, the majesty of the Creator. Though the question of salvation history and its possible relation to alien life is complex, Scripture's repeated attestations to God's sovereignty over the entire cosmos (e.g., Psalm 103:19) encourage believers to greet cosmic discoveries without fear. The humility prompted by humanity's small physical footprint in the universe can become a catalyst for deeper reverence and inquiry.

In sum, the era from Galileo to Hubble revolutionized humanity's place in the cosmic story. Earth, once viewed as the center of everything, is now understood as one planet among many. Observational data, from the structure of the solar system to the accelerating expansion of galaxies, implies a universe that is dynamic, ever-unfolding, and immense beyond ordinary comprehension. Far from closing the question of extraterrestrial life, these developments have brought it to the forefront of scientific and theological debate.

4.1.2 New Frontiers: Exoplanet Exploration

The First Exoplanets

While speculation about other worlds has existed for centuries, concrete evidence for planets orbiting stars other than the Sun did not arrive until the early 1990s. In 1992, astronomers Aleksander Wolszczan and Dale Frail announced the discovery of planets orbiting a pulsar (a rapidly rotating neutron star). Pulsars are typically hostile environments for life, but this breakthrough opened the door to finding exoplanets—planets beyond our solar system.

Then, in 1995, Michel Mayor and Didier Queloz detected a planet around the Sun-like star 51 Pegasi. This discovery marked the first detection of an exoplanet orbiting a main-sequence star similar to our own. Named 51 Pegasi b, it was a "hot Jupiter"—a massive gas giant orbiting very close to its star. Its existence defied expectations based on our solar system's architecture, showcasing that planet formation can yield surprising outcomes. Astronomers soon realized that if they found one exoplanet, the cosmos could easily teem with them.

Methods of Detection

Multiple techniques have since been developed to identify exoplanets:

1. **Radial Velocity Method** By measuring slight wobbles in a star's motion caused by the gravitational pull of an orbiting planet, astronomers can infer the planet's mass and orbital distance. This method is highly effective for large planets in tight orbits, though improvements in sensitivity now allow detection of smaller, Earth-like planets as well.

2. **Transit Photometry** When a planet crosses in front of its host star, it dims the star's brightness by a minuscule amount. Sensitive instruments on telescopes can detect this dip, revealing the planet's size relative to the star. Repeated transits confirm the planet's orbital period. Spectroscopic analysis during transits can even indicate the chemical composition of a planet's atmosphere, offering clues to habitability.

3. **Direct Imaging** Capturing actual images of exoplanets is challenging because the host star outshines them by many orders of magnitude. Specialized techniques, such as coronagraphy, block the star's light to reveal faint objects around it. Though direct imaging remains difficult, advances in adaptive optics and space-based instruments have yielded pictures of a few exoplanets, primarily young gas giants.

4. **Microlensing** When a massive object (like a star with a planet) passes between Earth and a distant background star, the foreground object's gravity bends and magnifies the light of the background star. This short-lived event can reveal the presence of planets, even if they do not transit their host star. Microlensing is particularly sensitive to planets in wide orbits, complementing other methods.

Collectively, these techniques have confirmed thousands of exoplanets, with more candidates awaiting verification. They include rocky worlds only slightly larger than Earth, gas giants many times the size of Jupiter, and "super-Earths" that occupy an intermediate mass range. Some orbit in their stars' "habitable zones," where temperatures might allow liquid water on the surface—though the presence of water also depends on a planet's atmospheric composition and geological processes. Regardless, the sheer variety of exoplanets underscores that the cosmos does not lack creativity.

What Counts as Habitability?

A key consideration is whether exoplanets can support life as we understand it. Earth-based biology depends on liquid water, carbon-based chemistry, and stable energy sources. Scientists often look for planets orbiting at the right distance from their stars (the habitable zone), having sufficient mass to retain an atmosphere, and hopefully possessing conditions conducive to chemical complexity.

Yet, the scope of "habitability" might be wider than Earth's particular recipe for life. Studies of extreme microorganisms on our planet reveal that life can flourish in environments once deemed impossible—such as deep-sea hydrothermal vents, acidic hot springs, and Antarctic ice. If life on Earth can adapt to such extremes, exobiology (the study of potential extraterrestrial life) wonders if alien microbes (or more advanced organisms) could thrive under conditions vastly different from our own.

From a theological standpoint, this quest can be read in concert with verses affirming God's creativity. If Genesis 1:20–22 portrays waters teeming with living creatures at God's command, might not other cosmic "waters" or environments also harbor living processes? Science has yet to confirm such a possibility, but the principle of cosmic plurality resonates with long-standing Christian reflections on divine freedom in creation.

Merely finding a planet is the first step. The next frontier involves characterizing its atmosphere, surface, and potential biomarkers—substances like oxygen, methane, or other gases that, on Earth, arise through biological activity. Increasingly powerful observatories, both on Earth and in space, aim to detect these chemical signatures in exoplanet atmospheres. Should any future data strongly suggest biological processes, it would mark one of the most transformative discoveries in history.

While some in the Christian community might initially react with surprise or concern, many theologians and scientists see potential synergy with biblical themes of God's grandeur. The possibility of cosmic life might deepen our appreciation for the vastness of divine creativity. Precisely how this intersects with doctrines like the Incarnation or original sin remains a matter of speculation—best approached with humility and an acknowledgment that Scripture speaks to the human story primarily, but does not exhaustively describe all of God's works.

4.2. Our Celestial Neighborhood

4.2.1 Solar System Perspectives

The Sun: Our Local Star

Though overshadowed by the billions of stars in the Milky Way, the Sun remains our most critical reference point for life. Its fusion engine provides light and heat, making Earth habitable. Historically, many cultures worshiped the Sun as a deity; from a biblical viewpoint, however, the Sun is a created entity (Genesis 1:16), one among many luminaries formed to "govern the day." Modern astronomy classifies the Sun as a G-type main-sequence star—hardly the largest or brightest, yet a stable star with a lifespan of about 10 billion years.

The Sun's structure influences the entire solar system. It anchors planets in elliptical orbits, streams out solar wind that shapes planetary magnetospheres, and fosters conditions for phenomena like auroras. Understanding the Sun's properties helps us appreciate that stars, rather than being mere points of light, are dynamic systems with their own life cycles: birth in nebulae, long stable middles, and eventual death as white dwarfs, neutron stars, or black holes. If we want to speculate about the potential for life around other stars, comprehending our own star is foundational.

The Planets and Their Diversity

Our solar system contains eight major planets, each distinct. Mercury is a barren, airless world scorched by solar proximity; Venus, enshrouded by a thick, toxic atmosphere, is often called Earth's "evil twin"; Earth is the lone planet confirmed to harbor life; Mars, once more habitable, now shows evidence of ancient rivers and lost oceans. Beyond Mars lies the asteroid belt, a frontier of rocky debris, followed by the gas giants—Jupiter and Saturn—and the ice giants—Uranus and Neptune. Some dwarf planets, like Pluto, orbit in the Kuiper Belt and further into the scattered disk, hinting at a solar system that extends well beyond Neptune.

Planets and their moons present tantalizing possibilities for life. Jupiter's moon Europa, Saturn's moon Enceladus, and even Titan have subsurface or surface liquids that might host microbial life. Though Earth remains unique in its complex biosphere, these smaller worlds remind us that habitability could emerge in unexpected corners. Scientific missions, from the Voyager probes to current rover explorations on Mars, keep unveiling solar system wonders that challenge earlier assumptions. Each discovery broadens our sense of cosmic possibility, underscoring that Earth's story might be one among countless planetary narratives.

Comets, Asteroids, and the Cosmic Debris

Comets—icy bodies that release glowing tails when warmed by the Sun—act like time capsules. They contain primordial materials from the early solar system's formation roughly 4.6 billion years ago. Studying their composition offers clues about how water and organic molecules may have been delivered to Earth, possibly jumpstarting life's emergence. Similarly, asteroids showcase varied compositions—metallic, rocky, carbonaceous—and occasionally collide with planetary surfaces. Such impacts have shaped the solar system's evolution, including mass extinctions on Earth.

From a theological angle, the interplay of comets and asteroids resonates with biblical themes of dynamic creation. Rather than a static universe, Scripture portrays creation as imbued with potential and ongoing processes. Psalm 102:25–26 affirms that, though the heavens themselves "will perish," God remains eternal. This underscores a theological openness to cosmic change—stars, planets, and smaller bodies all exist under divine sovereignty yet follow natural laws that can lead to dramatic transformations.

The Edge of the Solar System

Far beyond Neptune lies the Kuiper Belt, home to dwarf planets like Pluto and Makemake, along with countless icy fragments. Even further is the hypothesized Oort Cloud, a vast spherical shell of cometary material extending, in theory, halfway to the nearest star. The existence of this massive reservoir of comets underscores how little we have explored. Earth-based observations and the occasional spacecraft flyby offer glimpses, but the outer reaches of the solar system remain largely mysterious.

For the curious Christian, this uncharted domain is a reminder that human knowledge, despite impressive advances, remains partial. If we cannot fully map our own cosmic backyard, how much more remains undiscovered in the galaxy at large? Biblical texts celebrating God's infinite understanding (Psalm 147:5) take on new resonance in the face of these unknown frontiers. Our solar system's complexity stands as a microcosm of the creativity that might be replicated, in diverse forms, elsewhere across the cosmos.

4.2.2 Galactic and Intergalactic Scales

The Milky Way: Our Galactic Home

If the solar system is our cosmic neighborhood, the Milky Way galaxy is our extended hometown. With an estimated 200 to 400 billion stars, the Milky Way measures about 100,000 light-years across. Our Sun sits in a suburban locale within one of the galaxy's spiral arms, approximately 27,000 light-years from the galactic center. Dark dust lanes, vast gas clouds, and dense star clusters mark the Milky Way's structure, visible as a diffuse milky band across Earth's night sky.

At the galactic center lies a supermassive black hole named Sagittarius A*. Its mass—over four million times that of the Sun—exerts gravitational influence on surrounding stars and gas. Giant molecular clouds spawn new stars, while older stars drift in the stellar halo or cluster in globular systems. This vast ecosystem of star birth and death, black holes, nebulae, and cosmic rays exemplifies the rich tapestry that a single galaxy can contain.

Despite centuries of stargazing, the Milky Way's full shape and extent remained elusive until radio and infrared astronomy allowed us to penetrate dust clouds. Today, we realize our galaxy is only one among many, each with its own structure, chemistry, and potential for harboring planetary systems. Reflecting on passages like Daniel 12:3—"Those who are wise will shine like the brightness of the heavens"— some believers see an allegory in the countless stars: each is a beacon in a cosmic tapestry, hinting at a divine purpose that spans far beyond human borders.

Neighboring Galaxies and Group Dynamics

Our galactic neighborhood includes Andromeda (M31), about 2.5 million light-years away, and the Triangulum Galaxy (M33), both members of the Local Group. This group encompasses over 50 galaxies, bound loosely by gravity. Andromeda is on a slow collision course with the Milky Way, expected to merge in roughly four to five billion years. Such interactions, while spanning astronomical eons, shape the cosmic environment. When galaxies collide, star formation can burst forth in gravitationally disturbed gas clouds, forging new stellar generations and, potentially, new planetary systems.

Further out lie galaxy clusters—gravitationally bound families of hundreds or thousands of galaxies. Clusters themselves often group into superclusters, forming filaments in a vast "cosmic web," with immense voids in between. The scale defies simple visualization; each step outward multiplies the mind-boggling sense of cosmic immensity. Yet, if the same laws of physics apply everywhere, we have reason to suspect that many of these galaxies host solar systems with Earth-like planets. Whether these worlds are inhabited remains unknown, but the sheer quantity suggests that even a tiny probability per planet could yield a multitude of life-bearing environments.

Dark Matter and Dark Energy

Modern cosmology grapples with mysteries that push understanding even further. Observations of galactic rotation curves indicate that visible matter (stars, gas, dust) accounts for only a fraction of a galaxy's total mass. An unseen component, dubbed "dark matter," exerts gravitational effects yet does not interact with electromagnetic radiation. Meanwhile, the universe's accelerating expansion is attributed to "dark energy," an enigmatic force that makes up nearly 70% of the cosmic energy budget. In total, ordinary matter comprises a mere 4–5% of the universe.

These findings highlight how much remains to be discovered. We stand in a cosmos where the majority of content is invisible, either because it does not emit light or because our theoretical frameworks are incomplete. Biblically speaking, one could draw parallels to the notion that "what is seen was not made out of things that are visible" (Hebrews 11:3), though this verse addresses creation's dependence on God rather than the specifics of dark matter. Nonetheless, the scriptural principle that much lies beyond human perception resonates with modern recognition that we barely grasp the fundamental nature of most cosmic matter and energy.

Cosmic Time and the Universe's Future

Beyond spatial immensity, the temporal aspect of the universe also stretches human comprehension. Current models suggest the cosmos is about 13.8 billion years old. In that time, cosmic expansion, star formation, and galactic evolution have shaped the environment in which life might arise. Stars burn their fuel, go supernova, and seed the next generation of stars with heavier elements—a process crucial for forming rocky planets and biological molecules. The future, on scales of billions of years, likely involves continued star formation in some regions while others grow cold as usable energy depletes. Galaxy mergers will reshape cosmic neighborhoods.

Such timelines challenge any notion that Earth's few thousand years of recorded history represent the entire cosmic narrative. For Christian believers, this extended timescale can be integrated with the biblical affirmation of God's eternal perspective: "For a thousand years in your sight are but as yesterday when it is past" (Psalm 90:4). The unfolding cosmic drama might serve as a backdrop for a divine plan that transcends human chronological boundaries. Whether or not we ever detect extraterrestrial intelligence, the universe's ongoing story invites a humility rooted in both scientific observation and theological reflection.

Conclusion

Astronomy and our expanding grasp of the universe's scope have radically reshaped humanity's conception of reality. From Galileo's telescopic glimpses of lunar craters and Jovian moons to the sophisticated measurements of exoplanet atmospheres and galactic collisions, each discovery has chipped away at parochial illusions. Earth is indeed special for us, and it remains the only confirmed cradle of life, but the cosmos it inhabits is vast beyond reckoning. Galaxy upon galaxy spreads out, each potentially brimming with planetary systems where life could exist in forms we have yet to imagine.

At the same time, the Christian tradition offers a lens through which these scientific revelations can evoke worship rather than despair. The biblical ethos, from Genesis to Revelation, often portrays creation as a testament to divine power and wisdom. While scriptural authors knew nothing of exoplanets or dark energy, their insistence that God created and governs "all things" aligns well with a universe that continually reveals new layers of depth and complexity. The question, "Are we alone?" therefore becomes not only a scientific puzzle but also a prompt for spiritual introspection. Might a God who names each star also people those stars with life? Or is Earth's biosphere a singular design?

Either way, the synergy between astronomy and faith rests on a common ground of wonder. A mind open to the possibility of a Creator can find, in cosmic immensity, a stirring symbol of divine magnitude. Conversely, scientific inquiry benefits from the humility and sense of awe that can motivate explorers to push the boundaries of knowledge. Astronomy, therefore, is more than data collection—it is a journey into the heart of existence, revealing vistas that kindle curiosity about our Creator as much as about ourselves.

Chapter 5: Faith and Science in Conversation

Humanity has always been curious about the heavens, and in modern times, scientific discoveries have accelerated our understanding of the universe at an unprecedented rate. From advanced telescopes peering at distant galaxies to robotic probes landing on other planets, the pursuit of knowledge about our cosmic surroundings has become a global endeavor. As these discoveries unfold, many people of faith ask how scientific insights align—or conflict—with religious convictions. Do new findings about potentially habitable exoplanets challenge the core tenets of Christianity or other religious traditions? Or does the vastness of space merely underscore the grandeur of the God many worship?

Over the centuries, theologians and scientists have engaged in debates that swing between conflict and concord. The "conflict thesis" gained traction in the 19th century, suggesting that science and religion were locked in perpetual battle. However, in more recent decades, a growing number of scholars argue for a model of complementary engagement: science offers insights into how the natural world operates, while faith addresses questions of purpose, meaning, and morality. In this chapter, we will explore these models in the context of our cosmic inquiry: "Are we alone?" How do science and faith converse—and potentially cooperate—to address this profound question?

5.1. Overlap of Worldviews

5.1.1 Complementary or Conflicting Narratives?

Shifting Paradigms in History

The relationship between faith and science has undergone multiple paradigm shifts. During the medieval era, natural philosophy—what we now call science—was often pursued by scholars who were deeply religious, studying nature as a means of understanding God's handiwork. Figures like Robert Grosseteste, Roger Bacon, and later Johannes Kepler, all operated within a theistic worldview. Their assumption was that the universe was coherent and lawful precisely because it was created by a rational God. This conviction emboldened them to experiment, measure, and theorize, believing that the cosmos could be studied systematically.

However, the Enlightenment brought growing secularization, championing human reason and empirical observation as the ultimate arbiters of knowledge. This shift did not inherently negate belief in God, but it did encourage people to think critically about religious claims that lacked verifiable evidence. Over time, some construed this approach to mean that faith was antithetical to reason—a stance culminating in the "warfare" narrative of the 19th century. Famous controversies, such as the Galileo affair (discussed in broad strokes in previous chapters), further solidified the impression that religious institutions resist scientific progress when it challenges long-held doctrines.

Yet, these tensions are not the whole story. Many Christian thinkers maintain that scientific inquiry can deepen faith by revealing the complexity and majesty of creation. For them, the question "Are we alone?" is not an attempt to undermine

God's uniqueness in forming humanity, but an invitation to marvel at the breadth of divine creativity. Far from being threatened by the potential existence of extraterrestrial civilizations, such believers view it as consistent with a God whose imagination and power surpass human understanding. This perspective aligns well with Scriptures that extol the limitless power and wisdom of the Creator (Psalm 145:3; Isaiah 55:8–9).

Defining Conflict and Complementarity

Scholars often propose several models to describe the interaction between science and faith:

1. **Conflict Model** Science and faith are inherently incompatible. Proponents argue that scientific explanations leave no room for the supernatural, rendering religious beliefs obsolete or irrational.
2. **Independence Model** Science and faith address fundamentally different domains of knowledge: science focuses on empirical facts, faith on spiritual truths. Thus, the two do not overlap enough to conflict.
3. **Dialogue Model** Science and faith intersect in certain areas—like ethics, origins, and purpose—encouraging conversation rather than isolation. They can enrich each other's understanding by sharing complementary insights.
4. **Integration Model** Here, science and faith are deeply interwoven, each shaping the other's framework. This approach posits that the natural order is best understood through a theological lens, and theology must stay informed by empirical discoveries.

When pondering alien life, the conflict model might claim that the potential discovery of extraterrestrials would refute "anthropocentric religion," proving that humanity is not the center of creation. The independence model would say that whether aliens exist is purely a scientific question, having little bearing on theology. The dialogue model suggests that any proof of other life forms would trigger important theological discussions—how would revelation or salvation extend to them? Finally, the integration model welcomes new discoveries as an expansion of what believers already understand about God's creative power, seeing each confirmed exoplanet or new star system as an ongoing testament to divine artistry.

Most Christians today fall somewhere between dialogue and integration, seeing both value and limits in scientific explanations, while maintaining that faith fills a dimension of human experience not addressed by data alone. These nuanced positions reflect the complexity of reconciling an ancient faith tradition with modern scientific advances. Indeed, the quest to find life beyond Earth provides a vivid arena for observing how these models unfold in real time. Debates over planet habitability, cosmic scale, and theological anthropology highlight the multifaceted ways in which science and faith intersect, confound, and sometimes illuminate each other.

Points of Mutual Enrichment

For believers drawn toward integration or dialogue, scientific studies of the cosmos can be deeply enriching:

- **Humility**: Recognizing Earth's minuscule size in a galaxy teeming with stars can bolster humility. Scripture commends humility (James 4:10), and acknowledging our cosmic smallness can align well with that mandate.
- **Wonder and Worship**: Observing planetary orbits, supernova remnants, or stellar nurseries can spark profound awe, resonating with biblical passages that praise God's majesty (e.g., Psalm 19:1–4).
- **Moral Reflection**: Scientific exploration raises ethical questions about how humanity should steward Earth, or interact (hypothetically) with other life forms if discovered. Faith traditions provide moral and ethical frameworks for addressing such questions, supplementing the data-driven approach of science.
- **Intellectual Inquiry**: Christianity has a rich intellectual heritage that values the pursuit of truth (John 8:32). When approached with openness, scientific

discoveries become occasions to refine, deepen, or even reformulate theological understanding, ensuring that faith does not stagnate.

In these ways, the faith-and-science conversation need not be a zero-sum contest of doctrines versus data. Instead, it can be a cooperative journey, one that respects the methods of science while seeking to discern the spiritual implications of cosmic immensity. For many Christians, this synergy culminates in an even grander view of God—one commensurate with the breathtaking scale of the universe modern astronomy reveals.

5.1.2 Methodological Differences

Science as a Method

Science, strictly defined, is a method for investigating natural phenomena. It relies on empirical observation, testable hypotheses, and reproducible experimentation. The scientific method proceeds by identifying a question, formulating a hypothesis, designing experiments or observations, collecting data, and drawing conclusions that either support or challenge the hypothesis. Peer review and replication are core components, ensuring that new ideas withstand rigorous scrutiny before gaining acceptance.

In the context of potential extraterrestrial life, science seeks observable evidence. Researchers examine exoplanet atmospheres for bio-signatures, analyze Martian soil for traces of past organic compounds, and scan radio signals for patterns indicating intelligence. Until conclusive data emerges, the question "Are we alone?" remains open. Scientists vary in their predictions: some see the universe as so vast and presumably bio-friendly that multiple civilizations are likely, while others emphasize the delicate conditions required for life and remain more skeptical. Either way, the scientific posture is cautious, evidence-driven, and slow to adopt definitive conclusions without robust data.

Faith as a Mode of Knowing

Faith traditions, particularly in Abrahamic religions like Christianity, operate with a different epistemic basis. While Christianity can embrace reason and evidence (Romans 1:20 speaks of God's attributes being "clearly perceived" in creation), it also relies on revelation—divine self-disclosure in Scripture, the person of Jesus Christ, and ongoing spiritual experience. Believers affirm truths that may not be empirically verifiable, such as the reality of a transcendent God, angels, or the resurrection of Jesus.

These beliefs often rest on historical documentation, communal tradition, personal conviction, and philosophical arguments rather than purely laboratory-based experimentation. Indeed, the biblical exhortation in Hebrews 11:1 describes faith as "the assurance of things hoped for, the conviction of things not seen." While some interpret this verse to mean that faith is blind trust devoid of evidence, others view it as pointing to a different *dimension* of evidence—testimony, spiritual insight, and a communal witness of divine action that transcends the scientific realm.

When reflecting on extraterrestrial life, faith communities might ask how God's redemptive plan could encompass unknown beings or whether cosmic-scale creation narratives open the door for life scattered across the stars. The scientific method, by contrast, demands tangible observation or detection to make definitive statements. There is no direct contradiction here, but each domain—science and faith—uses different approaches to explore reality.

Common Ground and Complementary Aims

Despite these methodological differences, science and faith share important commonalities:

- **Desire for Truth**: Both aim at understanding what *is* real. A religious believer seeks ultimate truth about God and existence, while a scientist pursues physical truths about how the universe operates.

- **Wonder and Curiosity**: Both are propelled by curiosity. The scientist wonders how cosmic phenomena work, the believer wonders about their meaning in a creation context. This sense of wonder can unite rather than divide.
- **Community and Tradition**: Science operates within a community of researchers, building on peer-reviewed literature and accepted paradigms (Thomas Kuhn's "normal science"). Faith communities rely on shared creeds, historical teachings, and interpretive traditions. Both spheres rely on communal consensus and tradition, albeit in different ways.
- **Revisability and Growth**: While some might argue that theology rarely changes, church history reveals doctrinal development over time. Likewise, science modifies its theories when new data emerges. Both are capable of growth, correction, and deeper insight.

In the conversation about extraterrestrial life, these shared values can foster a constructive dialogue. Scientists can remain faithful to empirical methods while inviting theologians to consider new data's implications for doctrines like the Incarnation or human uniqueness. Conversely, theologians can enrich scientific pursuits with ethical frameworks and existential reflection, sparing the scientific enterprise from moral or philosophical vacuums. Rather than seeing each other as adversaries, faith and science can function as conversation partners, unveiling different layers of truth about a universe that might harbor more mysteries than we can currently imagine.

5.2. Interpreting Biblical Texts in Light of Astronomy

5.2.1 Literalism vs. Contextual Understanding

The Complexity of Biblical Genres

One of the most debated areas in faith-and-science dialogue involves biblical interpretation. Scripture comprises diverse genres—poetry, narrative, prophecy, epistles—spanning centuries of authorship in ancient Near Eastern and Greco-

Roman contexts. Literalist readings sometimes treat every passage as a precise historical or scientific statement, whereas more contextual approaches read texts in their original cultural, linguistic, and literary settings.

For instance, the opening chapters of Genesis have often been at the center of creation debates. A literalist might see these chapters as a strict chronological account of cosmic origins in six 24-hour periods, concluding the universe is only a few thousand years old. A contextualist might read the same chapters as a theological narrative emphasizing God as Creator, humanity's dignity in the "image of God" (Genesis 1:26–27), and the goodness of creation—without demanding a modern scientific timeline. This difference in hermeneutics can lead to starkly divergent attitudes toward cosmological evidence and the potential for extraterrestrial life.

When confronted with the idea of billions of galaxies, each harboring countless stars, literalists might feel an urgent need to reconcile these numbers with a specific reading of the biblical text. Contextual interpreters, in contrast, may argue that Scripture's main thrust is theological rather than scientific, allowing them to embrace an ancient text's theological truths while affirming modern astronomy's findings. Notably, biblical references to "the heavens" (e.g., Psalm 115:16) can be seen as expansive rather than limited. If so, acknowledging the universe's enormous scale could, in the contextual view, deepen appreciation for the Creator's power rather than conflict with Scripture.

Case Study: The "Waters Above the Heavens"

A curious example arises in Genesis 1:6–7, which describes a "firmament" separating "waters above" from "waters below." In ancient cosmology, it was often assumed that there was a solid dome overhead holding back heavenly waters. Literalist interpreters may wrestle with how to reconcile this with modern meteorology and space science, often concluding that these waters refer to atmospheric vapor or poetic imagery. Contextual interpreters tend to see this passage as reflecting an ancient worldview that God used to communicate a deeper theological message: God established order in creation, separating elements for life's flourishing. In such a reading, the emphasis lies on divine sovereignty and purposeful structuring, not the physical layout of the cosmos.

Applying this principle to the question "Are we alone?" invites humility. If the biblical authors used the cosmological frameworks of their time to illustrate God's lordship, it does not necessarily limit us from discerning new truths about the universe's scope via modern astronomy. Nor must it force us to confine God's creative activity to Earth alone. A contextual hermeneutic can thus integrate current science with an understanding that Scripture is primarily about God-human relationships, moral imperatives, and salvation history, not a comprehensive astronomy manual.

Unity in Diversity

It is crucial to note that even within Christianity, believers span a wide spectrum from strict literalism to more flexible readings. While these interpretive differences can create internal disputes, they also reflect the broader tapestry of Christian thought. Many churches have become more accepting of "day-age" or "framework" interpretations that see Genesis 1 as a theological framework rather than a literal timeline. This opens up space to affirm the universe's age of roughly 13.8 billion years and the existence of myriad celestial objects. In doing so, faith in God as Creator remains intact while accommodating empirical data.

In the conversation on extraterrestrial life, a less rigid hermeneutic frees Christians to consider cosmic possibilities without feeling they betray Scripture's core messages. The biblical story of redemption, culminating in Christ's Incarnation (John 1:14), remains central, but the question of whether other life forms exist remains open, a domain where theology can dialogue with scientific findings. Literalist approaches can also find ways to reconcile new data, though it may require more interpretive gymnastics. Ultimately, the range of interpretive models underscores that the biblical text is living and active, applied anew in each generation as humanity's horizon of knowledge expands.

5.2.2 Cosmic Christology

The Universal Reach of the Incarnation

Central to Christian theology is the doctrine that God became incarnate in Jesus Christ for the redemption of humanity (John 1:14; Philippians 2:6–8). Traditional formulations emphasize Christ's death and resurrection as pivotal for saving a fallen human race, a narrative intimately connected to Earth's history. But how might this narrative extend if intelligent life exists on other planets? Would they require their own Incarnation events, or does Christ's singular incarnation have universal efficacy?

The New Testament occasionally alludes to a cosmic scope of Christ's reign. Colossians 1:16–17 states, "For by him all things were created, in heaven and on earth, visible and invisible... and in him all things hold together." Such verses have spurred theological speculation that Christ's redemptive work might apply beyond Earth-bound humanity. While Scripture does not address alien life directly, passages like Ephesians 1:9–10 speak of God's plan to "bring unity to all things in heaven and on earth under Christ." Could "all things" imply a cosmic dimension that includes other rational beings?

These reflections form the basis of what some theologians term "cosmic Christology." They propose that Christ is not merely the Savior of Earth but the center of a universal story. If other civilizations exist, they too may be subject to Christ's dominion, though we cannot say how redemption would look for them. Some draw an analogy to angels: they are non-human intelligences also under God's authority. If such spiritual beings relate to Christ, perhaps the same principle could apply to physical extraterrestrial beings. While speculative, these ideas offer a theological framework for welcoming future discoveries without dethroning Christ's central place in salvation history.

Fallen vs. Unfallen Worlds

A related question is whether alien races (if they exist) would share in the Fall described in Genesis 3. Christian tradition teaches that Adam's disobedience ushered sin into the human condition, requiring Christ's atoning sacrifice. But are hypothetical aliens "in Adam" as well, or might they be unfallen? C.S. Lewis, in his fictional *Space Trilogy*, imagined inhabited planets untainted by sin, continuing in their innocent worship of God. Other theologians wonder if multiple falls could have occurred across the cosmos, each requiring divine intervention.

Though purely hypothetical, these scenarios encourage reflection on the extent and nature of sin and redemption. Romans 8:19–22 describes the whole creation groaning under the weight of sin, awaiting redemption. Does this "whole creation" include distant galaxies? Or is it limited to Earthly creation and its immediate context? Without a definitive biblical text, Christians remain free to entertain various possibilities, guided by overarching doctrines of divine goodness, justice, and sovereignty.

The potential theological complexities highlight one reason why many Christians adopt a wait-and-see approach. While cosmic Christology remains a stimulating field, it need not be resolved prematurely. The overarching principle gleaned from Scripture is that all creation ultimately depends on God's sustaining grace (Hebrews 1:3), and Christ's work is presented as globally—and possibly cosmically—significant. Thus, if or when evidence of alien life surfaces, the Christian tradition has theological resources ready to interpret it.

Spiritual Implications of a Cosmic Christ

Even without direct evidence of extraterrestrials, considering cosmic Christology can deepen believers' spiritual lives. Contemplating a Christ enthroned over billions of galaxies can spark a sense of wonder akin to the Psalmist's awe (Psalm 8:3–4) at the scale of divine handiwork. This cosmic perspective might also humble anthropocentric tendencies, reminding Christians that God's love extends beyond any single culture, species, or planet. Such humility resonates with biblical teachings on the church's global mission (Matthew 28:19–20), only now extended metaphorically to a cosmic dimension—proclaiming the goodness of God not just to "all nations" but potentially to "all creations" wherever they might be found.

For many, this grand vision of a cosmic Christ does not undermine traditional faith; rather, it magnifies it. The Incarnation remains the pivotal moment in history, but that history is set against an unimaginably large stage. Far from diminishing the gospel's significance, the idea that the Creator of galaxies chose to step into human flesh can heighten the sense of divine compassion. It underscores that the God who fashioned star clusters and black holes also cares intimately about humanity's joys and sorrows. Thus, cosmic Christology can foster a deeper worship that embraces both the microscopic (our personal relationship with God) and the macroscopic (God's reign over a potentially teeming universe).

Conclusion

In this chapter, we discussed how faith and science can converse, rather than clash, in addressing the question, "Are we alone in this universe?" The conversation hinges on recognizing distinct yet complementary modes of inquiry. Science tests hypotheses about exoplanets, biosignatures, and cosmic evolution, illuminating the vast possibilities for life. Faith explores ultimate meanings, grounded in Scripture's witness to a Creator and Redeemer who reigns over "the heavens and the earth." Differences in methodology need not yield hostility; indeed, many have found that scientific discoveries about the universe's immensity strengthen rather than weaken their awe for God.

The path of dialogue or integration, rather than conflict, opens a robust space for Christian theology to engage new data. Interpreting biblical texts with sensitivity to genre and context allows believers to retain core doctrines while embracing the expanding cosmic picture. The concept of cosmic Christology, though speculative, offers a theological lens to view a universe that might be brimming with life beyond Earth. Even if we never find definitive evidence for extraterrestrials, considering the possibility can enrich our appreciation of God's grandeur.

Ultimately, the conversation between faith and science, as it pertains to potential alien life, underscores deeper themes relevant to all Christians:

1. **Humility**: Faced with cosmic vastness, humans recognize their smallness, aligning with the biblical call to humble ourselves under God's mighty hand (1 Peter 5:6).
2. **Wonder**: Scientific revelations about exoplanets, galaxies, and the universe's age can ignite a profound wonder that the psalmists and prophets anticipated— an invitation to worship "the Maker of heaven and earth" (Psalm 146:6).
3. **Compassion**: A cosmic perspective can enlarge our hearts toward caring not just for our planet and neighbors but also for the potential dignity of any life, wherever God may have created it. Such compassion echoes biblical mandates to love our neighbor (Mark 12:31) and to steward creation responsibly (Genesis 2:15).
4. **Hope**: Whether or not life exists elsewhere, the Christian story culminates in a renewed creation (Revelation 21–22). The cosmic dimension of that hope suggests that no corner of the universe is beyond God's redemptive scope.

Engaging these themes fosters a faith robust enough to stand alongside modern science, welcoming new questions rather than silencing them. In doing so, believers can confidently join the broader human quest to understand the cosmos, guided by both reverence for God's Word and respect for the investigative tools of science.

Chapter 6: Angels, Heavenly Hosts, and Non-Human Intelligence

When Christians reflect on non-human intelligences, they often turn first to angels and the wider "heavenly host" depicted throughout the Bible. Angels are God's messengers, worshippers, and sometimes warriors, presented in both Old and New Testaments as beings separate from humanity yet deeply involved in the unfolding of salvation history. Whether they appear at crucial junctures in Israel's story or announce Jesus's birth to shepherds, angels act as a bridge between the heavenly realm and earthly affairs.

6.1. Biblical Accounts of Angelic Beings

6.1.1 Messengers of God

Varied Roles and Appearances

In both Hebrew and Greek, the terms for angel—*mal'akh* in Hebrew and *angelos* in Greek—literally mean "messenger." Scripture consistently portrays angels as heralds and intermediaries between God and humankind. For instance, the angel Gabriel delivers momentous news in the Book of Daniel (Daniel 8:16; 9:21) and later announces the births of John the Baptist (Luke 1:13–19) and Jesus (Luke 1:26–38). In these episodes, angels serve God's communicative purpose, bridging the gulf between finite human understanding and divine intention.

Their forms vary throughout the Bible. Sometimes angels appear as ordinary men—so unremarkable that they are unknowingly hosted by humans, as when Abraham offers hospitality to three mysterious visitors at Mamre (Genesis 18:1–8). In other instances, their appearance is dazzling or fear-inspiring, prompting individuals to bow in awe or tremble in terror (Judges 13:6; Luke 2:9). These differing depictions suggest that angels can manifest in ways discernible to human senses, yet they belong to a dimension not constrained by the physical limitations of our world.

Guiding and Protecting

Angels also perform protective and guiding roles. The Psalmist proclaims, "He will command his angels concerning you to guard you in all your ways" (Psalm 91:11). Such verses bolster the concept of guardian angels, spiritual beings assigned by God to safeguard individuals or communities. In the New Testament, the Book of Acts provides an example: an angel rescues the apostle Peter from prison (Acts 12:7–11). While believers differ in how literally they interpret guardian angels, the notion remains embedded in Christian devotion, reflecting the broader biblical theme that God uses heavenly agents to accomplish His compassionate purposes.

Beyond personal guardianship, angels often direct historical events. Daniel 10 portrays a cosmic struggle in which angelic "princes" battle for or against the people of God—an image that suggests angelic involvement in shaping the destinies of nations. Such narratives highlight that angels are not merely peripheral characters but integral to the biblical vision of how God orchestrates world affairs. Though invisible to ordinary perception, their influence weaves through the fabric of salvation history, reinforcing the idea that creation encompasses more than the material.

Significance for the Question "Are We Alone?"

When we wonder if we are alone, angels remind us that Scripture posits at least one category of non-human intelligence. Of course, angels are not aliens in the usual sense: they are spirit beings, presumably without physical biology, who serve God and sometimes interact with humankind. Yet their existence helps us conceptualize that God's creation spans multiple orders of beings—He is not limited to fashioning only humans. While angels do not confirm or deny the existence of extraterrestrial life, they do show that Christian theology has long accepted the notion that intelligent existence transcends humanity.

6.1.2 Heavenly Worship and Service

Heavenly Host: The Wider Company

Beyond individual angels, the Bible often refers to a "heavenly host" or "hosts of heaven" (e.g., 1 Kings 22:19; Psalm 103:20–21), a term that encompasses multitudes of spiritual beings worshipping and serving God. This host can include angels, archangels, cherubim, seraphim, and other orders not fully defined in Scripture. For example, Isaiah's vision (Isaiah 6:1–4) features seraphim worshipping around God's throne, proclaiming His holiness. Ezekiel's visions (Ezekiel 1; 10) describe living creatures with awe-inspiring forms—often identified as cherubim—beneath the divine throne-chariot. Revelation 5:11–12 depicts "myriads of myriads" of angels praising the Lamb.

These passages reinforce the idea that heaven is a realm teeming with life, albeit spiritual rather than physical. If humans often imagine "Are we alone?" strictly in terms of cosmic solitude, Scripture's answer is "No," even apart from any speculation about alien life. The heavenly host testifies to a reality where worship, service, and heavenly activity continue beyond earthly boundaries. This host functions as a cosmic liturgy, exalting God and enacting His will throughout creation.

Angelic Hierarchies and Roles

Church tradition, influenced by Scripture and theological reflection, has proposed hierarchies of angels. Pseudo-Dionysius the Areopagite's work, *The Celestial Hierarchy* (5th–6th century), famously categorized them into nine orders—seraphim, cherubim, thrones, dominions, virtues, powers, principalities, archangels, and angels—though this detailed taxonomy lacks direct biblical proof-texting for each rank. Still, the biblical hints of archangels (Jude 1:9, 1 Thessalonians 4:16) and varying titles for angels support the notion of varied roles within the heavenly host.

For instance, the archangel Michael appears as a chief prince contending for Israel (Daniel 10:13; 12:1) and leading heavenly armies (Revelation 12:7). Gabriel, as noted, is often a herald. Though Scripture does not always systematize these distinctions, the existence of different angelic functions underscores a rich spiritual ecosystem—one in which God delegates tasks to His celestial servants. These hierarchical structures reflect an ordering reminiscent of the complexities we find in creation, where diversity and interdependence weave a tapestry of function and purpose.

Implications for Cosmic Scale

In exploring the concept of cosmic scale, angels (and the wider heavenly host) evoke a sense of innumerability. Revelation 5:11 speaks of "ten thousand times ten thousand" angels around God's throne. While this is symbolic language, it suggests an uncountable throng. Christians sometimes link this imagery to the vast number of stars visible in the cosmos: if God's creation of spiritual beings is so abundant, it parallels the almost incomprehensible physical abundance of galaxies and stellar systems. In that sense, the heavenly host, like the starry firmament, hints at the boundless generosity of God's creative act—spanning realms physical and spiritual.

6.2. The Spiritual Realm Beyond Earth

6.2.1 Differences Between Angelic and Human Existence

Nature and Abilities

A key distinction between humans and angels lies in their nature. While human beings are embodied creatures, angels are often described as incorporeal spirits who can take on physical form as needed (Hebrews 1:14 describes angels as "ministering spirits"). Consequently, angels do not marry or reproduce (Matthew 22:30), nor do they rely on food, water, or atmospheric conditions for survival. Their existence transcends the usual biological constraints that define earthly life.

In theological terms, humans bear the "image of God" (Genesis 1:26–27), which implies moral agency, relational capacity, and rational thought. Angels, too, possess intelligence and will, as suggested by Scripture's portrayal of some angels rebelling (2 Peter 2:4; Jude 1:6). Nonetheless, the extent of their free will, knowledge, or emotive range remains partly mysterious. Angels seem to grasp divine realities more fully than humans do (e.g., Luke 1:19), yet they are not omniscient or omnipotent (Psalm 103:20 underscores they obey God's commands).

Mortality vs. Immortality

Humans, since the Fall, experience mortality; our bodies age and die (Genesis 3:19; Romans 5:12). Angels, conversely, appear to possess a form of immortality in their spiritual state—Scripture does not mention angels dying in the conventional sense. Even fallen angels (demons) persist until a final judgment (Matthew 25:41; Revelation 20:10). This divergence in mortality raises intriguing questions about how spiritual beings fit into the broader creation narrative, which is otherwise marked by physical decay and entropy.

Yet biblical eschatology teaches that faithful humans will eventually receive resurrected bodies (1 Corinthians 15:42–

44), entering an existence akin to angels in some respects (Luke 20:36). This suggests that redeemed humanity will share certain attributes with angels—immortality, direct communion with God—without losing our uniquely human identity. In short, angels and humans remain distinct orders of creation, but Christian theology envisions a future where the boundary between earthly and heavenly forms of life is transformed by God's renewing work.

Relevance to Extraterrestrial Speculation

These distinctions remind us that spiritual beings differ fundamentally from the hypothetical biological extraterrestrials sought by modern astronomy. Angels do not inhabit planets or rely on carbon-based chemistry. They exist in a realm beyond standard physical constraints. Thus, while angels affirm that non-human intelligences exist, they do not confirm that the cosmos abounds with "flesh-and-blood" alien societies. Instead, they enrich our understanding of God's creative range, showcasing that intelligence and life need not always mirror human biology. This perspective opens theological space for the possibility that God could create other embodied intelligences as well.

6.2.2 Unseen Dimensions

Biblical Insights on the Unseen

Throughout Scripture, references to invisible realms abound. Elisha's prayer in 2 Kings 6:17 reveals an entire mountain filled with horses and chariots of fire, otherwise invisible to human eyes. In the New Testament, Paul teaches that believers wrestle "not against flesh and blood" but against "the rulers, authorities, cosmic powers over this present darkness" (Ephesians 6:12), implying spiritual forces at work behind the scenes. Such verses illustrate that biblical authors recognized layers of reality beyond the immediate physical environment.

For modern readers, this concept can be compared loosely to higher dimensions in contemporary physics—hypothetical spaces beyond our three-dimensional experience. While the analogy is not exact, it underscores that reality may be more complex than what our senses can detect. Biblical authors do not employ scientific language, but their portrayal of invisible angelic hosts, demonic forces, and divine presence resonates with the idea that creation includes aspects beyond standard empirical measurement. This leads to a theology that is open to unseen cosmic or spiritual "topographies."

The Intersection of Realms

At times, Scripture shows these spiritual dimensions intersecting with human history in tangible ways. Jacob's ladder (Genesis 28:12) presents a vision of angels ascending and descending between heaven and earth, signifying a continuum rather than a rigid barrier. Similarly, the Book of Revelation frequently describes heavenly realities that impact earthly events—judgments, worship scenes, and angelic proclamations that shape the course of history (Revelation 8–9; 19:1–10).

If the question "Are we alone?" focuses solely on physical neighbors in the cosmos, the biblical witness might redirect us to consider how spiritual intersections occur right in our midst—undetected except through divine revelation or extraordinary circumstances. The Christian worldview thus envisions a multi-layered cosmos in which the visible and invisible coalesce under God's sovereignty. From this vantage point, angels and other heavenly hosts remind us that our quest for cosmic companionship should not ignore the spiritual realm already revealed.

Misidentifications and Modern Folklore

In contemporary culture, some have speculated that biblical descriptions of angels or "fiery chariots" are actually ancient accounts of extraterrestrial visitation. While this "ancient astronaut" theory has gained popularity in certain circles, it lacks strong scholarly support and generally conflicts with how biblical texts define angels in theological contexts. Scripture's authors consistently present angels as divine messengers, loyal or rebellious spiritual beings, rather than advanced flesh-and-blood extraterrestrials.

Nevertheless, these modern reinterpretations highlight a broader point: humans often sense a reality beyond the visible. Whether that sense is channeled into biblical convictions about angels, science-fiction imaginations of aliens, or esoteric theories about cosmic visitors, it resonates with a longing for connection to beings beyond ourselves. The biblical perspective upholds that angels are real but categorically distinct from hypothetical aliens, cautioning us against conflating the two in ways that neglect the primary spiritual and redemptive functions angels hold in Christian belief.

6.3. If Extraterrestrial Life Exists: Distinguishing Spiritual vs. Physical Realms

6.3.1 Potential Confusions and Clarifications

Angels vs. Aliens

Given the biblical presentation of angels as powerful non-human intelligences, some Christians question whether advanced extraterrestrial species—if discovered—might be angels in disguise. Conversely, others might wonder if the angels described in Scripture were actually aliens misunderstood by ancient authors. Both hypotheses conflate categories that Scripture and science approach differently.

From the biblical standpoint, angels are defined primarily by their relationship to God and their spiritual essence. They do not inhabit other solar systems as biological organisms but exist in a sphere that intersects with the physical world at God's direction. Aliens, as conceptualized by science, would be physical life forms emerging through natural processes on another planet. These distinctions in ontology (spiritual vs. physical) and origin (directly created as spiritual beings vs. presumably evolving in a cosmic environment) mark clear differences.

Hence, a Christian theology that accepts the reality of angels can still remain open to the possibility of alien life without conflating the two. Angels serve a theological role in worship, revelation, and cosmic governance under God, whereas aliens—if found—would represent biological neighbors sharing the universe with humanity. Both sets of beings would, in principle, be under the Creator's domain, yet their modes of existence and purpose differ significantly.

Demonic Deception?

Another concern sometimes raised is whether reported alien encounters or "extraterrestrial phenomena" might be demonic deceptions. Scripture does warn that demons can manipulate perceptions (2 Corinthians 11:14), sometimes masquerading as "angels of light." This leads some to interpret unexplained aerial phenomena or alleged alien abductions as spiritual interference rather than genuine visitors from space.

While Christian tradition indeed acknowledges deception by fallen angels, caution is warranted before labeling all mysterious encounters demonic. Many sightings are ultimately explained by natural or technological factors, and the small percentage that remain unexplained do not necessarily equate to demon activity. The theological priority is discerning truth, staying faithful to biblical teaching about spiritual warfare while remaining open to scientific explanations. Ultimately, an unverified UFO sighting is a poor foundation for claiming either divine or demonic presence.

6.3.2 Theological Openness to Further Creation

A Spectrum of Created Life

The existence of angels and heavenly hosts highlights that God's creative capacity is not limited to terrestrial, carbon-based organisms. Indeed, Scripture identifies multiple categories of life—humans, animals, angels, and presumably other spiritual entities (cherubim, seraphim, etc.). This multiplicity can cultivate openness to the idea that God might have fashioned additional categories of sentient, physical life beyond Earth.

The canonical texts do not explicitly affirm or deny extraterrestrial biology. Instead, they situate humanity as a unique steward and image-bearer on Earth while acknowledging that God's creative power spans realms visible and invisible (Colossians 1:16–17). Thus, the same God who populates the heavens with myriad angels could, in principle, populate the stars with myriad species. The presence of angels does not prove the existence of aliens, but it erodes any assumption that a single form of life is all God would create.

Cosmic Drama and Redemption

If we posit the existence of non-human intelligences—whether angelic or extraterrestrial—Christian theology points to Christ's cosmic lordship (Colossians 1:18–20). For angels, Scripture is clear: they are called to serve and honor God, some having remained faithful, others fallen from grace (Revelation 12:7–9). For hypothetical aliens, theology can only speculate on whether they might be "unfallen," needing no redemption, or "fallen," requiring a form of divine intervention akin to what God provided humanity through Christ.

Although angels and aliens are distinct categories, they converge in the sense that both reflect a creation not circumscribed by human limitations. In either case, God's redemptive plan extends as far as His creation does. Where and how that redemption unfolds remains a mystery. Yet the biblical narrative consistently depicts God as intimately involved with all aspects of creation—from the forging of galaxies to the spiritual battles among angelic hosts. This expansive vision fosters a humility that reminds believers: the scope of God's works may surpass human comprehension (Isaiah 55:8–9).

6.4. Practical Reflections

6.4.1 Spiritual Formation and Angelic Awareness

Balancing Fascination and Reverence

Interest in angels can become a double-edged sword. On one hand, Scripture encourages believers to acknowledge the role of angels as ministering spirits. On the other, Paul warns against worship of angels (Colossians 2:18), cautioning that excessive obsession can distract from Christ. For spiritual formation, a healthy perspective includes gratitude for angelic guardianship, awe at God's manifold creations, and ultimate devotion to the Creator rather than His messengers.

In an age fascinated by the supernatural—whether ghosts, spirit guides, or alleged alien contacts—Christians can offer a biblical framework that neither dismisses the existence of non-human powers nor elevates them above their proper station. This balance fosters reverence for the God who alone deserves worship. By seeing angels as loyal servants in God's cosmic household, we learn humility and reliance on divine providence. At the same time, we guard our hearts against misguided adoration of spiritual beings or unwarranted fear of malevolent forces.

Discernment in Spiritual Encounters

Given biblical warnings that Satan and demons can disguise themselves (2 Corinthians 11:14), believers are called to discern spiritual encounters. The New Testament suggests testing spirits (1 John 4:1), aligning experiences with scriptural truths. If an apparition or messenger contradicts essential Christian doctrines, it cannot be from God. This standard applies to any phenomenon—angelic, demonic, or (in theory) extraterrestrial—purporting to bring new revelation.

Such discernment does not require suspicion of every spiritual experience. Genuine angelic intervention often accompanies biblical faithfulness, humility, and alignment with God's redemptive aims. But a healthy skepticism ensures that believers remain anchored in Scripture and the Holy Spirit's guidance, protecting against deception. Thus, acknowledging angels as real does not mean accepting all extraordinary claims at face value.

6.4.2 Stewardship of Creation and Cosmic Responsibility

Earthly Stewardship as a Training Ground

The presence of angels and the possibility of other non-human intelligences can broaden our sense of cosmic responsibility. Genesis 1:28 tasks humanity with stewarding Earth—caring for animals, ecosystems, and the planet's well-being. If God entrusts us with such tasks on Earth, might our moral accountability extend beyond our immediate sphere? Scripture does not specifically say, but some theologians argue that responsible dominion on Earth prepares us for roles in a "new heaven and a new earth" (Revelation 21:1), where the fullness of God's kingdom will reconcile all creation.

Angels, for instance, are portrayed carrying out divine governance in spiritual realms (Daniel 10). Perhaps, in our redeemed state, humans too will share in cosmic governance, though the details remain obscure (1 Corinthians 6:3 suggests we will "judge angels," implying a future authority or partnership). If so, treating Earth responsibly now is a form of training for potential cosmic tasks, fostering virtues of empathy, humility, and service that might apply to interstellar contexts if the saga of redemption includes other worlds.

Ethical Considerations for Contact

While direct contact with aliens is speculative at this stage, Christian ethics, shaped by biblical principles of love (Mark 12:30–31) and justice (Micah 6:8), can already inform how we might approach such encounters. Just as angels demonstrate that God invests dignity in non-human beings, so might we extend dignity to any extraterrestrial life we meet—treating them not as curiosities to exploit but as neighbors bearing the imprint of the Creator.

Even if we never discover biological aliens, reflecting on this possibility fosters an outward-looking faith that acknowledges creation's vastness. Angels embody divine care and purpose beyond purely human concerns, suggesting that God's plan embraces a cosmic horizon. In turn, believers are challenged to adopt a mindset of stewardship that respects all life, whether terrestrial or hypothetical. This outlook resonates with the biblical refrain that God's mercies are "over all his works" (Psalm 145:9).

Conclusion

This Chapter has guided us through the biblical landscape of angels, heavenly hosts, and non-human intelligences of a spiritual nature. In the grand tapestry of Christian thought, angels stand as an enduring testament to the truth that we are not alone—there are realms beyond our immediate perception, filled with beings who serve, worship, and enact God's will. While these spiritual entities differ profoundly from the biological aliens contemplated by astronomy, they expand our vision of a universe teeming with life forms that surpass human understanding.

From their roles as messengers and protectors to their continuous worship before God's throne, angels underscore the multifaceted nature of creation. They remind us that God's creative impulse extends far beyond human confines, embracing both physical and spiritual dimensions. Indeed, the biblical drama includes not just earthly protagonists but invisible hosts that shape history and declare God's glory. In that sense, angels represent an integral bridge between the question of cosmic solitude and the reality of a populated spiritual cosmos.

Distinguishing angels from hypothetical extraterrestrial life is crucial: angels inhabit a spiritual realm and serve divine purposes, whereas extraterrestrials, if they exist, would presumably be biological creatures subject to astrophysical laws. Yet these distinctions do not diminish angels' significance for our broader inquiry. They show that Christian theology has always accommodated the possibility of non-human intelligences, reminding believers not to be unduly surprised if the universe proves more populous than anticipated.

Moreover, the angels' ceaseless worship and service to God mirror the greater truth that all creation—visible and invisible—finds its origin and destiny in the Creator's design. The New Testament's cosmic Christology (Colossians 1:16–20) resonates with this theme, envisioning Jesus's sovereignty over every realm, whether on Earth, in heaven, or possibly among the stars. Hence, if future discoveries reveal extraterrestrial civilizations, they would join a cosmic stage already populated by spiritual beings who declare God's holiness and partake in divine missions.

In practical terms, the doctrine of angels fosters humility, reverence, and discernment. It calls Christians to be aware of spiritual realities, grateful for angelic guardianship, but always centered on Christ as the ultimate revelation of God. It also invites a sense of responsibility: if the cosmos includes angels and possibly other creatures, believers bear the call to steward Earth faithfully and adopt a moral posture open to all forms of God's creation. Whether in the spiritual realm or in a galaxy far away, the question "Are we alone?" finds its richest answer in the biblical affirmation that the Maker of heaven and earth has fashioned a cosmos of profound depth and variety—one that summons us to worship, wonder, and wise stewardship under the reign of the Almighty.

Chapter 7: If Extraterrestrial Life Exists

The notion that humans may not be the only rational creatures in the universe has enticed imaginations for centuries. With the advent of exoplanet research, astrophysics, and astrobiology, the question "Are we alone?" looms large in both scientific and public discourse. For people of faith, however, the question transcends data collection: it touches on doctrines of creation, redemption, and humanity's place within God's cosmic plan.

No single biblical passage offers a definitive statement on alien life. Nonetheless, Christian theology has often wrestled with conceptual frameworks large enough to include possibilities beyond immediate human experience. Whether discussing angels, cosmic redemption in Christ, or the inexhaustible breadth of God's creative power, believers have long recognized that God's handiwork could exceed our current understanding.

7.1. Theological Considerations

7.1.1 The Image of God and Other Life Forms

Defining Imago Dei

Central to Christian anthropology is the concept of *imago Dei*, the belief that humans are created in the image of God

(Genesis 1:26–27). While theologians debate the precise meaning of this image—whether it entails rationality, moral agency, relational capacity, or the divine mandate to steward creation—most agree it is a mark of distinction that grants human life intrinsic worth and a unique calling in God's economy.

If intelligent extraterrestrials were discovered, believers would naturally ask whether they, too, bear the image of God. Scripture nowhere confines *imago Dei* to Earth alone, yet it clearly affirms that humanity is uniquely fashioned for a relationship with the Creator. Could there be multiple species who share this relational capacity? If so, might they be equally beloved by God, or might they reflect the divine image in a way distinct from humans?

Expanding or Preserving the Concept

Several theological pathways might be proposed:

1. **Universal Image**: In this view, *imago Dei* could be universal to all rational, moral agents in the cosmos. The biblical language about God creating "all things" (John 1:3) might be understood as inclusive of any intelligent species capable of knowing and loving God. This perspective underscores God's impartiality (Romans 2:11) and the possibility that multiple species could reflect the divine image in their own culturally or biologically distinct ways.
2. **Human-Exclusive Image**: Alternatively, some may argue that *imago Dei* applies specifically to Homo sapiens, grounded in the historic narrative of Adam and Eve. In this scenario, extraterrestrials, however intelligent, would not be *imago Dei* in the same sense but could still possess dignity as part of God's broader creation. Proponents might invoke biblical references to humanity's unique role in creation (Psalm 8:4–8) or the Incarnation's specificity in a human context (John 1:14).
3. **Tiered or Analogous Image**: A middle path posits that *imago Dei* for humans might not be exactly

replicated in extraterrestrials, yet they could bear an analogous relationship to God. They might have their own covenant or divine relationship, revealing the Creator's multifaceted engagement with different life forms. This notion harmonizes with biblical passages indicating diverse relationships between God and various creatures (e.g., Job 38–39 portrays animals each under divine care but not all in the same way).

Any of these views raises profound questions: Does the Incarnation in Christ remain humanity's unique redemption event? Could there be parallel redemptive histories for other species? Or might the Cross extend in some mysterious way to them as well? Though Scripture does not answer such specifics, the *imago Dei* discussion invites believers to hold fast to humanity's distinct, biblically attested role while staying open to the idea that God's creative and relational capacity might transcend Earthly bounds.

Practical Implications

How believers approach the question of *imago Dei* for aliens carries immediate ethical weight. If aliens are recognized as image-bearers, they deserve the same moral respect we accord other humans—a point that would shape how we interact with them should contact occur. Even if they are not deemed *imago Dei* in the precise human sense, they could still possess intelligence, emotions, and moral value, warranting cautious and respectful engagement. This underscores that theology is never merely abstract; in a scenario of interstellar contact, how we interpret the image of God would influence diplomatic, cultural, and even evangelistic strategies.

7.1.2 Salvation in a Cosmic Context

The Question of Sin

One longstanding debate among Christian thinkers is whether other intelligent races would share in humanity's fallen condition. Romans 5:12 indicates that sin entered the world through one man, Adam, and that "death spread to all men because all sinned." Yet this text does not explicitly address cosmic reach. Could it be that Adam's disobedience affected only Earth, leaving other species unfallen? Or might the entire cosmos be groaning under the same bondage (Romans 8:19–22), implying that alien life also suffers from the fractured state of creation?

Speculative though it may be, this issue impacts how we envision God's redemptive plan. If an extraterrestrial race has never fallen, they would not need atonement in the same way humanity does. They might be akin to the unfallen angels, perpetually aligned with God's will. Conversely, if they share in some version of original sin or moral defect, they too would require deliverance. In the latter case, do they participate in Christ's redemptive work, or might God have made a separate redemptive covenant with them?

The Universality of Christ's Work

Colossians 1:16–20 and Ephesians 1:10 emphasize Christ's cosmic lordship and reconciliation of "all things" in heaven and on earth. These passages form a scriptural foundation for what is sometimes called cosmic Christology, suggesting that Jesus's Incarnation, death, and resurrection have a scope beyond humanity alone. If that is true, it may include countless star systems and any beings dwelling there, even if they remain unknown to us.

Some theologians propose that if aliens are fallen, Christ's single sacrifice remains sufficient for all creation (Hebrews 10:10–12). The question of how they learn about or receive this salvation remains open—just as angels, for instance, are said to rejoice in human redemption (Luke 15:10), yet do not experience redemption themselves. Alternatively, others speculate about multiple Incarnation events, a theory that C.S. Lewis fictionalized in his *Space Trilogy*. While such ideas can spark controversy, they also highlight the vastness of God's creative freedom. From a biblical standpoint, the precise mechanics are not detailed, leaving believers to trust that the "Judge of all the earth" (Genesis 18:25) will do what is right.

The Enduring Mystery

Ultimately, how salvation might apply to extraterrestrial life remains a mystery. The biblical narrative focuses on human redemption through Christ, reflecting the immediate context of Earth's fall and covenant history. Yet Scripture does not limit God's reach, nor does it state that no other rational beings exist. Thus, Christians need not see potential alien life as rendering the Bible obsolete. Rather, it might invite deeper awe at the possibility that God's redemptive plan is even more expansive than we imagined.

In practical terms, any contact with alien beings who exhibit moral awareness would prompt urgent theological reflection. Churches might grapple with whether to share the gospel with them or whether they already stand in communion with God. Debates might mirror the early Church's struggles over Gentile inclusion (Acts 15), though on a cosmic scale. Regardless, the underlying principle is that the God revealed in Christ is not threatened by the vastness of creation; indeed, Scripture consistently portrays Him as Lord over all (Psalm 103:19).

7.2. Ethical and Pastoral Questions

7.2.1 Human Identity and Humility

Decentering Humanity

For centuries, the notion that Earth was the cosmic center prevailed in Western thought, supported by both philosophical and theological convictions. Copernicus and Galileo challenged that notion astronomically, yet many believers still assume a functional anthropocentrism—humanity is God's main focus. The discovery of extraterrestrials would force a reevaluation of that assumption. Far from diminishing the significance of humanity, it might encourage an honest humility, aligning with biblical passages that underscore human smallness before God's expansive creation (Psalm 8:3–4).

Such humility does not equate to insignificance. Though physically small, humans hold an elevated role in the biblical narrative, as indicated by Scripture's emphasis on covenant, prophets, and ultimately, the Incarnation of the Son of God as a human. Thus, a truly biblical posture might hold these paradoxical truths together: on one hand, we are finite, fragile creatures in a gigantic cosmos; on the other, we are intimately loved by the Creator. If other species share that love, it need not invalidate God's engagement with us. Rather, it broadens our perspective on how profoundly God loves life.

Pride, Fear, and Openness

The possibility of contact with advanced civilizations often triggers speculation about their technological might. Would they be benevolent or malevolent? Such concerns can devolve into either paranoia (worrying they'll subjugate us) or arrogance (assuming our spiritual insight outstrips theirs). A biblical approach might counsel caution without fear, recalling 2 Timothy 1:7, which states God gave us a spirit "not of fear but of power and love and self-control." Faith suggests that if God permitted such an encounter, it would occur under divine sovereignty.

Still, caution is warranted. Pride might tempt us to see ourselves as spiritual experts, presuming we must "evangelize the aliens" without first listening to their own knowledge of the Creator. Conversely, fear might cause us to erect barriers or respond aggressively, reminiscent of human conflicts driven by xenophobia. A posture shaped by Christian virtue would cultivate humility, empathy, and readiness to learn, even while discerning truth in light of Scripture.

7.2.2 Missional Implications

Sharing the Gospel… Universally?

One of the most pressing questions for many Christians is how to approach evangelism if intelligent aliens exist. The Great Commission (Matthew 28:18–20) commands believers to make disciples of "all nations." Would "nations" metaphorically extend to other planetary communities? Or is that an unwarranted leap, given Jesus's immediate context? The text itself does not clarify this cosmic dimension.

Some might argue that if a species is unfallen, they have no need for the gospel. Others hold that all moral creatures might benefit from understanding Christ's redemptive work, whether or not they share human guilt. The example of angels, who rejoice in the gospel (Luke 15:10) yet do not require forgiveness of sins, could illustrate that learning about God's work among other creatures can deepen cosmic worship. Hence, presenting the story of Jesus—His life, death, and resurrection—could be an act of cosmic testimony, not necessarily an attempt to "convert" beings who may already be living in divine fellowship.

Cultural Sensitivity and Contextualization

If Christians were to carry their message beyond Earth, cultural contextualization becomes exponentially complex. Throughout history, missionaries have striven to express the gospel in ways that respect local languages and customs. Engaging an entirely different biology, language system, or cognitive framework might require imaginative leaps we can scarcely fathom. The principle of incarnational ministry— entering another culture humbly, building trust, and learning from that culture—would be vital. Scripture emphasizes that Jesus Himself took on flesh and dwelt among us (John 1:14), suggesting God's preference for personal engagement over distant proclamations.

Practically, we would need to discern whether an alien society has a concept of divinity, morality, or spiritual longing analogous to human religiosity. If they do, bridging that gap might be possible; if not, new paradigms for communication might be required. Interstellar mission work, if it ever became feasible, would challenge the Church to embody the humility and servanthood Jesus modeled, reaffirming that the gospel transcends ethnocentric or geocentric limitations.

Partnership vs. Imposition

Evangelistic fervor must also be tempered by love and respect. Historically, some Christian missions to Earth's diverse cultures were marred by colonial attitudes. The possibility of engaging an alien civilization would underscore the need to avoid paternalism. Instead, believers could approach contact as an opportunity for mutual discovery: sharing what we know of Christ's redemptive love, while also learning how another species understands creation's purpose or divine mysteries.

This posture resonates with Paul's approach in Athens (Acts 17:22–31), where he built upon the Athenians' existing spiritual framework to introduce them to the "unknown God." A cosmic parallel might exist if we found alien religious traditions. The guiding principle would be to exemplify the love of Christ (John 13:34–35), rather than seeking power or exploitation. Perhaps such mutual respect could lead to a more genuine form of cosmic fellowship, reflecting the biblical vision of unity in diversity.

7.3. Pastoral and Practical Responses

7.3.1 Preparing Congregations for Discovery

Education and Theological Flexibility

Although the reality of extraterrestrial discovery remains hypothetical, it is not too early for churches and seminaries to address the topic. Education can prevent panic, skepticism, or confusion if evidence arises. Such education involves basic astronomy, exoplanet research, and astrobiology, as well as the biblical and theological frameworks we have explored. By fostering theological flexibility, congregations can adapt to emerging data without feeling that core doctrines are threatened.

Leaders might create small groups or workshops discussing how cosmic discoveries—past and future—interface with Christian faith. Scripture study can highlight texts like Psalm

19:1–4, Colossians 1:16–20, and Romans 8:19–22, which frame creation's vast scope and ongoing redemption. This approach encourages believers to see potential extraterrestrial life not as a crisis but as a further unveiling of God's inexhaustible creativity.

Encouraging a Posture of Wonder

Pastoral guidance can also channel curiosity into worship. Encountering new worlds or life forms, even if only through telescopic data, can stoke awe. Like the psalmist who proclaimed, "When I look at your heavens… what is man that you are mindful of him?" (Psalm 8:3–4), believers can respond with humility and gratitude. Whether or not we find conclusive proof of alien life, the quest itself deepens appreciation for the cosmic stage God has made. Sermons and teachings can integrate that wonder, steering believers away from fear or dogmatic rigidity.

7.3.2 Navigating Controversies and Fears

Addressing Doctrinal Anxiety

Some believers may worry that discovering aliens undermines the Bible's authority or the uniqueness of Christ. Pastors and theologians can reassure them that Scripture focuses on human redemption without negating the possibility of other forms of life. They can point to historical examples of Christian thought adapting to new realities, such as the Copernican shift, which did not demolish faith in God but refined understanding of how Earth fits into creation. Emphasizing God's transcendence over all creation can mitigate fears that new knowledge might dethrone divine sovereignty.

Maintaining Unity in Diversity of Opinion

Within any faith community, opinions on alien life will vary. Some will eagerly embrace the notion; others will remain skeptical or dismissive. Maintaining church unity in the face of disagreement is vital. Romans 14 provides a model for navigating disputable matters, urging believers not to "quarrel over opinions" (Romans 14:1). Whether we consider extraterrestrial life likely or unlikely, we can extend grace to those who differ. Since Scripture does not dogmatically define the question, the church can foster an atmosphere of respectful dialogue, focusing on shared convictions about God's character and mission.

Balancing Faith and Conspiracy

Church leaders might also have to address fringe theories or conspiracies about government cover-ups of alien life. While it is unwise to mock people's curiosities, it is equally important to encourage discernment and evidence-based inquiry. Christians can model thoughtful engagement, considering plausible scientific information while avoiding sensationalist claims. By affirming intellectual honesty and biblical wisdom, believers can steer away from extremes that hamper constructive discussion.

7.4. Living with Mystery and Hope

7.4.1 Embracing the Unknown

Scripture testifies to a God who transcends human understanding (Isaiah 55:8–9). Throughout the biblical narrative, key figures such as Job and the prophets grapple with mysteries they cannot fully resolve. The question of extraterrestrial life, likewise, remains shrouded in uncertainty. While the search for biosignatures on distant exoplanets or radio signals from advanced civilizations continues, definitive proof has yet to surface. Christians can affirm that a posture of waiting, akin to Advent expectation, can be spiritually fruitful. We are invited to dwell in humility, trusting that God's purposes, whether cosmic or terrestrial, unfold in His timing.

Rather than forcing tidy conclusions, believers can hold the tension between biblical revelation and scientific possibilities. If evidence arises, the church will adapt; if not, it remains a meaningful exercise in theological reflection that enlarges our sense of wonder. In this way, the question "Are we alone?"

becomes a catalyst for deeper meditation on God's sovereignty and creativity.

7.4.2 Testimony to a Grandeur Beyond Measure

Whether aliens exist or not, the sheer scale of the universe testifies to a grandeur that resonates with biblical themes of God's majesty. Passages like Job 38–41 remind us of creation's intricacies beyond our comprehension, culminating in a vision of God's unmatched power. In Romans 11:33, Paul exclaims, "Oh, the depth of the riches and wisdom and knowledge of God!" If the cosmos contains civilizations countless light-years away, that depth only grows more astounding.

Thus, the Christian response need not be apprehension, but worship. This perspective sees potential alien life not as a threat to faith, but as a possible further dimension of creation's chorus praising the Maker. It calls believers to a cosmic humility, a readiness to be surprised, and a confidence that, as the late Christian author C.S. Lewis wrote, "God is no fonder of intellectual slackers than of any other slackers."

Conclusion

This chapter has explored the theological, ethical, and pastoral implications if extraterrestrial life were to be confirmed. Themes such as the image of God, the scope of salvation, and the nature of human identity would come to the forefront, challenging believers to integrate new discoveries into a long-standing biblical worldview. Ethical questions—ranging from how we might treat alien life to how we might evangelize—would require careful thought rooted in love, humility, and the example of Christ.

Far from invalidating the Christian faith, the prospect of cosmic neighbors might deepen it. Humanity's role in the biblical drama, centered on the Incarnation and redemption, would still stand, yet within an expanded horizon that reveals more fully the magnitude of God's creative power. In practice, the church can prepare through education, fostering a spirit of openness and reverence for God's mysteries. Such preparation might mitigate fear or doctrinal anxiety, enabling believers to greet any confirmed discovery with wisdom, compassion, and worshipful awe.

Ultimately, the question "Are we alone?" remains unanswered scientifically, and Christians can hold it as an open, generative query rather than a divisive one. Whether or not advanced beings roam distant star systems, Scripture's affirmation that God "determines the number of the stars; he gives to all of them their names" (Psalm 147:4) invites us to trust in a Creator whose knowledge and care surpass our finite perspective. As we contemplate exoplanets, potential life forms, and cosmic scales, we return to the unchanging truth that the One who set galaxies in motion is also the One who knows every hair on our heads (Matthew 10:30). In that confidence, we can stand poised for discovery—or accept solitude—knowing that neither scenario exceeds the bounds of our ever-present, all-sustaining God.

Chapter 8: Philosophical and Existential Reflections

Humanity has long gazed at the skies, pondering whether the star-filled expanse contains other life. Even apart from the more technical debates of astronomy and theology, the sheer immensity of the cosmos rouses questions about our purpose, identity, and destiny. If the cosmos is indeed empty of other rational beings, what does that imply about human uniqueness—or perhaps cosmic loneliness? Conversely, if we find ourselves in a universe buzzing with intelligent civilizations, how might that reshape our sense of significance?

These questions are not purely academic. They strike at the heart of how we see ourselves as individuals, communities, and as a species. They beckon us to confront existential issues: the nature of consciousness, the search for meaning in a seemingly indifferent environment, and the possibility that our lives are part of a story stretching far beyond Earth's horizon. Philosophers, poets, and theologians alike have wrestled with these themes, whether or not they explicitly reference extraterrestrial life.

In this chapter, we will examine two major threads. First is the discussion surrounding the so-called "anthropic principle" and the idea of cosmic fine-tuning, which raises profound philosophical and theological implications. Second is the exploration of existential questions—loneliness, purpose, and meaning—that color how we respond to the possibility that Earth is unique or, alternatively, that we share the cosmos with countless others. As we reflect on these topics, we will see how the Christian tradition offers a framework that can welcome wonder, endure doubt, and inspire hopeful engagement with an ever-expanding cosmic vista.

8.1. Anthropic Principle and Fine-Tuning

8.1.1 Cosmic Constants

Philosophers and cosmologists frequently reference the "anthropic principle" when speaking of how the universe appears astonishingly calibrated for life. This principle notes that various physical constants—such as the gravitational constant, the speed of light, Planck's constant, and the cosmological constant—must fall within extremely narrow ranges in order for complex structures, including stars, galaxies, and ultimately life, to emerge. If these constants were even slightly altered, matter might not clump into galaxies, stellar fusion might never occur, or chemical complexity might collapse. Thus, from a purely scientific perspective, the coincidence of these precise parameters has prompted serious reflection on whether the universe is "designed" or whether we simply happen to exist in a cosmic lottery that, against all odds, produced our conditions.

Philosophically, the anthropic principle asks why these laws and constants are so seemingly "fine-tuned." Some see it as circumstantial; the only reason we notice this fine-tuning is because we exist in a universe that supports observers. If the universe did not have these conditions, we would not be around to ponder them. This is sometimes referred to as the "weak anthropic principle"—a tautology stating that intelligent beings find themselves in a universe that permits intelligence. Others invoke a "strong anthropic principle," suggesting that the cosmos must be constructed in a way to eventually produce observers. On that view, it is not mere coincidence but something woven into the fabric of reality.

Theological Resonances

Christian thinkers, among others, have long seen echoes of purposeful design in the harmony of nature. Passages like Psalm 19:1–2 speak of the heavens declaring God's glory, while Romans 1:20 suggests that creation reveals aspects of God's attributes. Although these texts do not detail physical constants, they affirm that God's handiwork can be discerned in the orderliness of the world. The fine-tuning discussion aligns with that perspective, proposing that a life-friendly cosmos might point to a Mind behind the universe.

Still, such arguments remain open to multiple interpretations. Some might treat cosmic fine-tuning as strong evidence for a Creator who set up the laws of nature to allow for life's emergence. Others caution against an overly simplistic "God of the gaps," warning that fine-tuning may be partially explained by future scientific discoveries—or even by speculative multiverse theories, which propose that our universe is one among many, each with different fundamental constants. These debates illustrate a broader intersection between science and philosophy: Is the cosmos fundamentally the product of random chance, or is it the outworking of deliberate intention?

8.1.2 Debates in Cosmology

Fine-tuning arguments lead to lively debates over whether the universe's apparent precision is best accounted for by purposeful design or natural processes:

1. **Design Hypothesis**: Proponents argue that the simplest explanation for such remarkable specificity is an intelligent Designer. Observations like the narrow window for nuclear fusion in stars or the balance between matter and antimatter reinforce the idea that the cosmos is delicately calibrated. In theological

terms, this view resonates with the biblical affirmation of God as an intentional Creator (Isaiah 45:12).

2. **Multiverse Theories**: Another approach posits that our universe is but one among a vast (or infinite) ensemble of universes, each with different laws and constants. In that case, it is not surprising that at least one universe would randomly exhibit life-permitting conditions—this is simply the one we inhabit. While some see multiverse theories as speculative, others find them philosophically appealing, negating the need for a singular cosmic design.

3. **Unknown Natural Laws**: A third path suggests that science has yet to uncover deeper laws that necessarily generate the constants in question. If future theories like quantum gravity or string theory unify known forces, the values we call "fine-tuned" might be inevitable outcomes. Here, the question shifts: is there an underlying rational structure that compels these constants to be just so, and might that structure, too, be indicative of a cosmic mind?

Implications for Human Meaning

Beyond the technical details, fine-tuning discussions impact how humans interpret their place in the universe. If the cosmos seems "set up" for life, that can foster a sense of being invited into a purposeful creation. However, if cosmic coincidences are purely random or part of an uncountable set of universes, humans might feel more inconsequential. These differing stances shape how individuals grapple with meaning and significance: is there something special about rational beings in a cosmos seemingly crafted for their emergence, or are we ephemeral flukes whose existence is no more ordained than that of any cosmic debris?

The Christian tradition typically leans toward the first interpretation, emphasizing the purposeful nature of God's creative act (Genesis 1:1–2). Yet that does not negate the possibility of cosmic vastness or multiplicity. Many believers hold that God's design could incorporate both fine-tuning and vast cosmic diversity, with each thread weaving together a tapestry that ultimately glorifies its Maker. Thus, the anthropic principle and debates around fine-tuning open a philosophical gateway to reflect on cosmic teleology, the notion that the universe is oriented toward life, discovery, and perhaps communion with the divine.

8.2. Loneliness and Purpose

8.2.1 Individual and Collective Significance

One of the starkest existential questions arising from our cosmic exploration is whether humanity is truly central or merely peripheral. On an individual level, each person grapples with feelings of meaninglessness when confronted by the overwhelming scale of galaxies, dark matter, and potentially countless stars. On a collective level, the human species might likewise question if we are "just another organism" in a cosmic ocean or if we occupy a unique place in the fabric of reality.

Personal Identity in a Vast Cosmos

From a Christian perspective, biblical texts suggest that God cares intimately for individuals. In Matthew 6:26, Jesus reminds His listeners that the Father watches over the birds, concluding that humans hold even greater value. Psalm 139 portrays a God who knows each person's inward parts, underscoring that no one is lost in the immensity of creation. This theological framework counters existential despair by affirming that personal significance does not hinge on cosmic scale but on relational standing with God.

Nevertheless, existential philosophers have often highlighted the tension between human aspirations for meaning and the apparent indifference of the universe. Figures like Albert Camus described life as "absurd" when the cosmos offers no transcendent response to human longing. Even if such perspectives differ from Christian hope, they articulate a widespread sentiment: the bigger the universe becomes, the more individuals may feel dwarfed by its silence. This sense of cosmic loneliness can provoke anxiety or a crisis of identity.

Christians who integrate existential insights might affirm that, although the cosmos is vast, love—both divine and human—can bestow a sense of purpose that outstrips mere physical dimensions. If we see ourselves as participants in a cosmic story orchestrated by God, we can preserve a sense of dignity even within an overwhelming environment. Thus, existential reflection need not plunge believers into nihilism; rather, it can highlight the fragile yet precious condition of life, spurring us toward gratitude and compassion.

Humanity's Collective Mission

At a collective level, some philosophers argue that the discovery of a vast, seemingly cold universe unmoors societies from older geocentric narratives. Historical shifts—from the Copernican revolution to modern astronomy—often challenged religious or cultural assumptions about Earth's centrality. While we need not repeat those historical debates here, it is worth noting that contemporary discussions about exoplanets and cosmic expansion intensify the question of whether humanity holds a special place or a global mission in creation.

In Christian thought, humanity is tasked with stewardship of the Earth (Genesis 1:28). But if the cosmic scope extends well beyond our planet, do we have a cosmic calling, or is our mission primarily local? Might the breadth of creation simply accentuate the magnitude of God's domain rather than enlarge our responsibilities? Opinions vary. Some see potential obligations to any other life forms if contact is established, while others maintain that our calling remains Earth-focused, defined by caring for our immediate environment and each other. Either way, cosmic perspectives can refine how we understand communal destiny, either inspiring fresh visions of unity or prompting humility as we acknowledge our finite sphere of influence.

8.2.2 The Human Drive for Connection

Yearning for Companionship

Whether we consider the possibility of alien life or angels (discussed in other contexts), humans demonstrate a deep longing for connection beyond themselves. This drive for companionship undergirds everything from personal relationships to grand cosmic dreams of encountering other civilizations. On a psychological level, we are social creatures seeking belonging; on a spiritual level, many yearn for communion with something transcendent. The question "Are we alone?" can be seen as an external projection of this internal quest for relationship.

Should it turn out that Earth is the only cradle of intelligence, some worry that cosmic isolation might breed existential dread. Yet from a Christian vantage point, companionship is not limited to human or extraterrestrial relationships— communion with God is deemed paramount (John 15:4–5). As Augustine famously wrote, "Our hearts are restless until they find rest in you." Even if the cosmos harbors no other advanced species, believers find solace in a God who promises nearness and ultimate fulfillment (Psalm 34:18; James 4:8). Philosophically, this implies that human loneliness is not absolute if one recognizes divine presence.

Dialogical Anthropology

Another angle is the concept of "dialogical anthropology," which posits that human identity is shaped in relationship not only with other people but also with the Creator or the Ultimate Reality. Martin Buber's *I and Thou* depicts the highest form of relationship as one that transcends objectification and moves into an encounter with the "Eternal Thou." While Buber was not Christian, his framework can converge with Christian thought, suggesting that real "dialogue" with the divine can satisfy the deepest relational yearnings.

In the cosmic context, the absence of alien contact would not negate the possibility of spiritual dialogue with God. Conversely, discovering other civilizations might open further forms of relationship, revealing new dimensions of the social, moral, and spiritual tapestry. Existential reflection, therefore, anchors human well-being not only in the recognition that we are social creatures but that the longing for connection ultimately finds expression in something or someone beyond ourselves, whether that be God or, hypothetically, cosmic neighbors.

8.3. The Search for Meaning in a Vast Universe

8.3.1 The Tension of Discovery

Anticipation and Perpetual Incompleteness

Philosophically, the ongoing pursuit of cosmic knowledge encapsulates a tension: each discovery (a new exoplanet, a cosmic structure, or an emerging theory) can intensify the sense that we are on the verge of unveiling a grand secret. Yet every advancement raises new questions, perpetuating a cycle of incomplete understanding. This dynamic resonates with the biblical idea that creation continually points beyond itself, reflecting a glory that humans can taste but never fully grasp (Psalm 145:3).

Some philosophers view this perpetual incompleteness as the essence of human progress. We find meaning in the journey—striving to map the cosmos, decode nature's laws, and possibly find life beyond Earth. Indeed, the Christian concept of "seeking" resonates with biblical admonitions: "Seek, and you will find" (Matthew 7:7). Nevertheless, ultimate fulfillment may not come solely from external discoveries but from an internal reorientation to what is ultimate or divine. The interplay between outward exploration and inward reflection characterizes the existential quest: we look to the stars, yet we also must look within.

Beauty, Terror, and the Sublime

The vastness of space can elicit contradictory feelings. On one hand, there is awe at the grandeur—gorgeous nebulae, graceful spirals of galaxies, or the shimmering arc of the Milky Way. On the other, cosmic phenomena such as black holes or supernova remnants provoke a sense of dread or smallness. Philosophers from Edmund Burke to Immanuel Kant used the term "sublime" to denote experiences that transcend beauty or pleasantness, evoking awe mixed with a kind of fearful respect.

Contemporary reflections on the sublime in astronomy emphasize how cosmic vistas exceed our capacity to domesticate them. For Christians, the sublime can point to the biblical notion of "the fear of the Lord," which does not imply terror in a cruel sense, but reverential recognition of God's majesty (Psalm 111:10). Thus, the cosmos itself can serve as a theater of the sublime—an existential sign that creation is larger, older, and more wondrous than our finite minds can contain.

8.3.2 Awe and Spiritual Reflection

Awe as a Catalyst for Worship

Existential discussions often revolve around "awe," an emotion bridging wonder, admiration, and humility. Awe arises in the face of something far greater than ourselves, be it moral virtue, natural beauty, or cosmic immensity. From a Christian standpoint, awe is not an endpoint but a gateway to worship. Biblical voices in the Psalms and Prophets repeatedly call for reverence in response to God's works. Psalm 33:8 proclaims, "Let all the earth fear the Lord; let all the people of the world revere him."

In a modern age saturated with scientific data, the spiritual potential of awe remains potent. Observing that the cosmos might be billions of years old and boundless in extent can deepen the sense of encountering a realm that dwarfs human concerns, thereby provoking heartfelt reverence. Philosophically, this stands as an antidote to nihilism: rather than concluding that bigness erases significance, many find that it magnifies the sense that we are caught up in a reality exceeding our comprehension—an invitation to worship the One behind it all.

Awe can also spur ethical and existential transformation. The experience of wonder may shift priorities, leading individuals to reflect on virtues like humility, gratitude, and stewardship. In a cosmic context, one might be prompted to see earthly life in a new light, more precious than ever given its apparent rarity. Some Christians interpret this impetus as a call to "walk humbly with your God" (Micah 6:8), cultivating compassion for fellow humans and responsibility for the environment. Philosophically, the concept of "transcendence" also plays a role, suggesting that awe invites us to step beyond self-centeredness into a broader sphere of awareness.

8.4. The Problem of Evil and the Universe

8.4.1 The Larger Theodicy

No existential reflection would be complete without addressing the problem of evil and suffering in a universe that believers claim is overseen by a benevolent Creator. Traditional theodicies wrestle with why a good God allows pain and moral wrongdoing. Expanding this question to cosmic proportions raises fresh complexities: if the universe hosts billions of galaxies, does that imply billions of potential sites for suffering? Or if we alone bear moral responsibility, how do we explain natural disasters on Earth or cosmic cataclysms like supernovae that can obliterate entire star systems?

Some propose a "greater good" or "soul-making" theodicy, arguing that adversity fosters virtues that would not otherwise emerge. In cosmic terms, the forging of heavier elements in supernovae, essential for planetary life, requires violent cosmic processes. Philosophically, we might interpret these processes as part of an unfolding tapestry, where destruction and creation interweave. Yet, this explanation may not fully quell the emotional weight of tragedy, especially when extended to hypothetical suffering on other worlds if such beings exist.

Biblical tradition does not shy away from the mystery of suffering. Books like Job depict cosmic wonders—stars, creatures, and meteorological phenomena—while acknowledging that human perspectives on divine governance remain limited. Job 38–41 portrays a Creator intimately involved in nature's drama, sometimes beyond human comprehension. From this vantage point, cosmic scale does not diminish God's care but highlights the gulf between divine omniscience and human finitude. The Christian tradition finds ultimate resolution in Christ's redemptive suffering (Romans 8:18–22), yet that does not erase the perplexities of present agony. Extending these complexities to a cosmic plane accentuates the depth of the problem: if other worlds experience pain, would God's plan encompass them as well?

8.4.2 The Cross and Suffering

A specifically Christian reflection sees the Cross as a point where God enters into suffering rather than remaining aloof. Though the scope of Christ's atonement is usually discussed in relation to human sin, the cosmic dimension of biblical passages (Colossians 1:20) hints that the redemptive act has broader implications. Philosophically, this means that the confrontation between divine love and evil might be more universal than we typically conceive. Even if we are not aware of other sentient beings, the principle remains that God's response to suffering involves solidarity and self-giving love.

For some, this perspective transforms the existential dread of a vast, possibly pitiless universe into a narrative where the Maker of galaxies also shoulders the weight of creaturely anguish. While such a stance does not solve the logical conundrum of evil, it offers an existential balm: a worldview in which infinite space does not reduce compassion to irrelevance but underlines the radical scope of divine empathy. That message can sustain hope in a cosmos that includes black holes and supernovae—where life emerges amid violent processes, yet can still partake in divine grace.

Conclusion

This Chapter, **Philosophical and Existential Reflections,** has traced the ways in which our understanding of the universe provokes deep questions about who we are and why we matter. From the anthropic principle and fine-tuning arguments, we see hints that the cosmos might be more than a cosmic accident. Yet the debates around design, multiverse theories, or unknown natural laws reflect a lively discourse where faith, reason, and speculation intersect. Similarly, reflecting on loneliness and purpose leads us to question whether vast cosmic expanses confirm human insignificance or highlight God's love for each person. The Christian tradition upholds that God's care persists no matter how immense or ancient the universe may be.

Further, the existential tension of discovery—swinging between awe and dread—reveals that cosmic exploration can magnify human yearning for connection, meaning, and moral direction. Philosophically, we wrestle with whether knowledge alone can satisfy that thirst. Christian faith adds a dimension of relationship with a Creator who surpasses the wonders of the cosmos. The notion of awe emerges as a potent force, prompting both worship and ethical responsibility. Whether we stand alone in the cosmos or share it with countless others, wonder can guide us toward deeper humility, compassion, and reverence.

Finally, the problem of evil magnified to a cosmic level intensifies the puzzle but also underscores the Christian conviction that God engages suffering redemptively. If the universe's scale can overwhelm us, it can also enlarge our vision of a God who intimately knows and cares for creation in all its complexity. For believers, the Cross stands as a testament that divine love penetrates even the darkest corridors of existence, offering hope for renewal and reconciliation on a scale we can scarcely fathom.

Chapter 9: Practical Faith in a Cosmic Context

9.1. Nurturing Awe and Worship

9.1.1 Prayerful Engagement with Creation

A core premise of Christian faith is that God is both transcendent over the cosmos and intimately involved in it (Jeremiah 23:23–24). When believers look to the heavens, they often experience what the Psalmist articulates: "The heavens declare the glory of God; the skies proclaim the work of his hands" (Psalm 19:1). Even so, in day-to-day life, many find it challenging to sustain that sense of cosmic wonder amid earthly concerns. One fruitful response is to cultivate deliberate practices that situate us within creation's vast expanse, enlarging our sense of worship.

Contemplative Stargazing One simple yet profound practice is setting aside time for contemplative stargazing. Whether in a quiet backyard, a church retreat center, or an observatory outing, gazing at the night sky can become an act of prayer. Rather than merely observing celestial objects, believers can frame the experience around gratitude and reverence. Passages like Isaiah 40:26—"Lift up your eyes on high and see: who created these?"—serve as prompts to shift from idle curiosity to purposeful adoration.

- **Practical Tip**: Provide star charts or smartphone apps to aid congregants in identifying constellations or planets, using these observations as moments to pray, "Lord, your handiwork is beyond my comprehension— let my heart respond with praise."

Nature-Themed Prayer Walks In rural or suburban areas, prayer walks that intentionally incorporate glimpses of the broader sky can remind believers of their place in a grand cosmic story. While the focus might be local creation—fields, streams, birds—pointing to the sky can anchor participants in a cosmic mindset. Each breath can become a reminder that we inhabit a world cherished by God. The prayer walk might also include readings from Scripture that highlight the divine craftsmanship of the universe (Job 38:1–7), blending the local environment with the cosmic vantage.

Pilgrimage to Astronomical Sites Though less common, some churches or groups arrange visits to places where the cosmic scale becomes more palpable—planetariums, large telescopes, or dark-sky reserves. These "pilgrimages" can be structured with guided devotions, each segment prompting reflection on a different aspect of God's creative power. For example, a planetarium show might showcase distant galaxies, after which participants read Psalm 8:3–4, "When I consider your heavens… what is mankind that you are mindful of them?" This juxtaposition can ignite deeper awe and a sense of humility that fosters worshipful hearts.

9.1.2 Worship in Light of Cosmic Splendor

Another dimension of practical faith lies in corporate worship. Congregations often incorporate references to creation in liturgy or song, but the cosmic breadth of God's handiwork can deepen these expressions.

Incorporating Cosmic Imagery in Worship Visual arts can play a powerful role in reminding worshipers of the universe's scope. Projected images of galaxies, nebulae, or star clusters during certain worship segments can nudge hearts toward adoration of the God who formed them. If technology permits, short videos or time-lapse footage of the night sky can precede reading passages such as Revelation 4:11—"You created all things, and by your will they existed and were created"—enhancing the sense that cosmic praise mirrors earthly praise.

Cosmic-Themed Hymns and Songs Many hymnals already contain creation-focused songs, yet churches can intentionally select or compose music that celebrates the vastness of God's dominion. Contemporary worship teams might write new anthems referencing exoplanets and galaxies, weaving modern scientific wonder into timeless theological truths. Traditional hymns like "How Great Thou Art" can be supplemented with new verses that highlight not only Earth's beauty but the expanses of interstellar space. The result is a worship tapestry that stands in awe of God's artistry on scales both intimate and immense.

Seasonal Observances Some congregations introduce "Season of Creation" elements into their liturgical calendar, dedicating several weeks to reflection on the environment and cosmic wonders. For a cosmic twist, a portion of the season could spotlight astronomy, referencing biblical passages that emphasize the heavens' testimony. Sermons might explore how scriptural authors perceived the sky, drawing parallels to modern astronomy and linking both to doxology. Through these seasonal observances, corporate worship offers ongoing reminders that the God of Scripture is not a provincial deity but the Lord of an ever-unfolding cosmos.

9.2. Equipping Churches and Communities

9.2.1 Educational Outreach

Knowledge about the universe can be transformative when applied through the lens of faith. Churches and communities that offer robust educational resources enable believers to embrace cosmic discoveries with confidence and curiosity rather than fear or skepticism.

Workshops and Seminars Weekend seminars or midweek classes can cover basic astronomy, exoplanet discoveries, and theology of creation. Local Christian astronomers or science educators might lead sessions explaining new developments—like the James Webb Space Telescope's findings—without overwhelming participants. Linking these scientific insights to biblical motifs (e.g., Romans 1:20 on perceiving God's invisible attributes through creation) can spark lively discussion. Providing space for questions avoids the pitfall of dogmatism and models the humility required for the ongoing journey of learning.

Bible Studies on Creation Passages Beyond single events, small-group Bible studies can delve into creation-focused texts—Genesis 1–2, Psalm 8, Romans 8:18–25—while weaving in contemporary cosmic perspectives. Participants might discuss how cultural assumptions have shifted from ancient times to now, comparing how biblical authors used available cosmologies and how we interpret the same passages today. Such studies do not need to present definitive positions on extraterrestrial life; rather, they can emphasize how Scripture's overarching message of God's majesty and care transcends any single cosmology.

Partnerships with Local Astronomy Clubs Some communities host amateur astronomy clubs or planetariums open to public collaboration. Churches might co-sponsor star parties or "Ask an Astronomer" nights that combine stargazing with reflective discussion. By creating a bridge between faith communities and scientific enthusiasts, believers can dispel misconceptions that religion and science must be at odds. These partnerships also demonstrate hospitality and intellectual engagement, inviting seekers or skeptics to witness a church that values scientific discovery as part of worshipful wonder.

9.2.2 Fostering Healthy Dialogue

In any congregation, opinions on cosmic questions may vary widely—from enthusiastic acceptance of new discoveries to cautious skepticism. Church leaders can shape environments where such differences become opportunities for growth rather than division.

Sunday School for All Ages Typically, Sunday school focuses on biblical narratives, doctrine, or ethics. But dedicated sessions on "Cosmic Christianity" can serve children, youth, and adults alike, providing age-appropriate lessons on astronomy, the possibility of extraterrestrial life, and how these topics intersect with core Christian convictions. For younger children, creative crafts and picture books about planets and stars can instill wonder, while teens might tackle more complex questions about science and faith. Adult classes can address philosophical or theological nuances. By embedding cosmic reflection in standard Christian education, churches signal that such topics are integral, not fringe.

Facilitating Q&A Forums Special Q&A forums or panel discussions let congregants pose tough questions—about evolution, exoplanets, the Bible's references to "the heavens," or the theological ramifications of alien life. Knowledgeable clergy and lay experts can respond graciously, emphasizing that many aspects remain open to prayerful exploration. The format encourages an honest exchange, helping participants see that Christian faith offers a wide tent for nuanced viewpoints and that it has historically adapted to expanding knowledge of the natural world.

Dialogue with Non-Christian Neighbors Cosmic questions often unite diverse individuals across religious or philosophical lines, as the night sky belongs to all. Churches can host interfaith dialogues or community events exploring universal questions: "What does the immensity of space reveal about purpose?" or "How do our different traditions respond to the possibility of alien life?" Such gatherings build relational bridges, fostering mutual respect. This approach exemplifies

1 Peter 3:15—offering a reason for hope with gentleness and respect—while acknowledging the cosmic stage we all share.

9.3. Cultural Engagement and Missional Perspective

9.3.1 Addressing Youth and Curiosity

Children and adolescents often experience unfiltered awe at the cosmos. They ask questions like, "Why are stars so big and far away?" or "Could people live on other planets?" Channeling that curiosity into a faith context can deepen their sense of wonder and guide them toward lifelong integration of science and spirituality.

Youth Groups and Science Clubs Church youth programs sometimes focus on fellowship, service, or Bible lessons. Supplementing these with science clubs or cosmic-themed projects can engage intellectually curious teens. They might build simple telescopes, track lunar phases, or study NASA missions. As they investigate, leaders can draw connections to biblical themes of God's creativity (Genesis 1:1–5) and humanity's role in stewarding knowledge (Proverbs 25:2). By demonstrating that faith endorses curiosity rather than stifles it, churches can nurture the next generation to be both scientifically informed and spiritually grounded.

Vacation Bible School or Summer Camps Vacation Bible School (VBS) or similar events can adopt cosmic themes— "Galactic Explorers," "Journey Through God's Universe," etc.—using decorations, games, and lessons that mirror the wonders of space. Scripture memorization might emphasize God's sovereignty over creation (e.g., Psalm 103:19). Activities could include building model solar systems or star charts, teaching that the same God who names the stars (Psalm 147:4) also knows each child by name. The result is a holistic approach that merges fun, education, and biblical truths about God's love manifest in a vast cosmos.

9.3.2 Interfaith and Ecumenical Collaboration

Many religious traditions have their own cosmic perspectives—whether rooted in Islamic, Jewish, Hindu, or Indigenous teachings. Collaborative efforts can highlight common ground in recognizing a transcendent dimension behind the physical universe.

Joint Forums on Cosmic Questions Working together with local synagogues, mosques, temples, or other Christian denominations can produce fruitful forums on cosmic wonder. Perhaps a roundtable discussion brings together rabbis, imams, pastors, and astrophysicists from different backgrounds to share how their traditions interpret the night sky. While doctrinal differences will remain, participants can unite in acknowledging the marvel of a universe that sparks spiritual reflection. By building relationships, believers also strengthen communal ties—an embodiment of Jesus's prayer for unity (John 17:20–23), extended beyond denominational lines to broader interfaith respect.

Shared Outreach in Global Issues Modern cosmic insights reveal Earth as a fragile oasis in an immense void. This vantage can unite religious communities in addressing global challenges—environmental care, resource stewardship, or peace-building. Recognizing that our "pale blue dot" thrives only under precise conditions (Acts 17:26–27) can inspire joint action to protect it for all people. In a sense, cosmic humility can foster solidarity, spurring collective efforts to honor the Creator by caring responsibly for creation, regardless of sectarian boundaries.

9.4. Ethical Implications in a Cosmic Framework

9.4.1 Environmental Stewardship on Earth

While cosmic questions often focus on "out there," they also illuminate moral duties "down here." The more we realize Earth's uniqueness, the more pressing it becomes to steward this planet. The biblical mandate for stewardship (Genesis 2:15) gains urgency when science underscores the fragility of life's conditions. Rising awareness of climate change, pollution, and biodiversity loss intersects naturally with a cosmic perspective that sees how extraordinary it is for a planet to host life.

Emphasizing Earth's Rarity Churches can integrate messages about Earth's rarity into sermons and small-group studies on creation care. Addressing deforestation, clean water initiatives, or climate action is not political activism alone but part of honoring God's gift of a life-supporting planet. Sermons might reference how exoplanet research suggests that Earth-like conditions are not guaranteed. Just as we marvel at cosmic wonders, we are called to guard the wonders at hand—forests, oceans, and ecosystems that sustain human communities and countless species.

Practical Green Initiatives Concrete steps might include church-sponsored recycling programs, energy audits to reduce the congregation's carbon footprint, or adopting solar panels if feasible. Educational events can highlight how daily lifestyle choices resonate with biblical values of stewardship. By framing these actions within a cosmic context, believers see Earth's stewardship as a tangible form of cosmic gratitude—responding to the God who fashioned a universe of abundance yet entrusted us with a unique biosphere.

9.4.2 Potential Responsibilities toward Extraterrestrial Life

While the notion remains speculative, many Christians have begun pondering ethical responsibilities if contact with extraterrestrial organisms—microbial or intelligent—ever occurs. A cosmic viewpoint invites reflection on how believers might approach the "neighbor" beyond Earth.

Principles of Dignity and Non-Exploitation Biblical ethics consistently advocate defending the vulnerable and avoiding exploitation (Micah 6:8; James 1:27). Extending such principles to alien life means treating them with respect, seeking mutual benefit rather than conquest. The parable of the Good Samaritan (Luke 10:25–37) exemplifies a love that crosses cultural or ethnic barriers. While cosmic contact might outstrip our present imagination, the guiding principle remains love of neighbor—where "neighbor" might someday include non-human persons.

Scientific Exploration Versus Colonial Mindset If future discoveries enable interplanetary or interstellar travel, the church could counsel caution against repeating historical mistakes of colonial expansion. Instead of imposing beliefs or exploiting resources, a Christlike approach would emphasize humility and listening first—paralleling inculturation strategies used by sensitive missionaries on Earth. The universal scope of God's kingdom (1 Chronicles 29:11) does not equate to human dominion or conquest but calls for service and peace-making. Should a cosmic frontier open, believers might champion respectful, ethically informed exploration consistent with biblical values of justice and love.

9.5. Emotional and Pastoral Considerations

9.5.1 Coping with Existential Doubts

The vastness of the cosmos can stir existential anxiety. Some believers may struggle with questions like, "Does my life really matter against galaxies spanning billions of light-years?" Pastoral care can address these concerns by rooting assurance in the biblical portrayal of a personal God who numbers the hairs on our head (Matthew 10:30).

Encouraging Transparent Conversation Small groups or pastoral counseling sessions can offer safe spaces for honest doubt. Building on scriptural examples—like Job's wrestling with cosmic mysteries or the Psalmist's cries of insignificance—pastors can validate such emotions while pointing to verses affirming God's intimate knowledge of each person (Psalm 139:1–16). The Christian tradition does not demand denial of existential angst but orients it toward the hope that God's sovereignty spans both cosmic distances and human hearts.

Guided Prayer and Meditation Spiritual practices like lectio divina (meditative Scripture reading) or centering prayer can help anxious believers find peace in God's presence. Passages like Psalm 46:10 ("Be still, and know that I am God") remind us that while the universe's immensity might overwhelm, silence before the Creator can ground us in unwavering love. Encouraging individuals to pair cosmic imagery—like a NASA photograph of a spiral galaxy—with meditative reflection on God's care can shift fear into reverent trust.

9.5.2 Providing Hope and Guidance

Alongside doubts, the cosmic perspective can spark wonder and yearning for transcendent purpose. Pastoral leaders can channel that energy into constructive spiritual growth.

Highlighting God's Immanence Though God transcends the cosmos, the Incarnation (John 1:14) demonstrates divine willingness to draw near in Christ. In pastoral preaching or counseling, reminding believers that the infinite Creator also walked among humanity fosters a paradoxical comfort. No matter how large the universe seems, it does not overshadow the reality that God's love was personally manifested in Jesus's life, death, and resurrection.

Reinforcing Eschatological Hope Scripture speaks of a "new heaven and a new earth" (Revelation 21:1), a future renewal of creation. While theological interpretations vary, the cosmic dimension of this promise indicates that God's redemptive plan includes more than just human souls. Pastors can reassure congregants that Christian hope extends beyond Earth's horizons, anticipating a cosmic restoration. Romans 8:19–22 pictures creation itself longing for liberation, implying that the fate of the universe is not random annihilation but renewal. Such eschatological vision can mitigate existential dread, affirming that the cosmic story culminates in God's triumphant grace.

Rituals of Cosmic Thanksgiving Some congregations incorporate communal acts to symbolize trust in God's overarching plan. For instance, a "Cosmic Thanksgiving" service might involve lighting candles for each major cosmic element—sun, moon, stars—accompanied by prayers praising God's provision. While we do not worship creation, acknowledging it in ritual form fosters gratitude for our place within a harmonious whole. This sense of gratitude can be psychologically and spiritually uplifting, reinforcing the conviction that we belong in God's vast creation.

Conclusion

This Chapter, **Practical Faith in a Cosmic Context,** illustrates how believers can actively integrate the enormity of the universe into their worship, education, ethical practice, and pastoral care. Far from viewing cosmic discoveries as irrelevant or threatening, Christians can harness them as catalysts for deeper wonder and worship. By adopting simple yet meaningful practices like contemplative stargazing or cosmic-themed liturgies, congregations foster hearts that resonate with the psalmist's proclamation, "How majestic is your name in all the earth!" (Psalm 8:1).

Equipping communities through educational outreach or partnerships with scientific institutions encourages a culture of inquiry tempered by reverence, demonstrating that faith and reason can thrive together. Engaging youth with cosmic themes ensures the next generation grows up seeing no dichotomy between a robust Christian faith and an expansive scientific worldview. Culturally, cosmic perspectives can fuel interfaith dialogue and reinforce stewardship of Earth, our fragile yet cherished habitat.

Ethical considerations broaden in cosmic reflection, reminding believers that the call to love one's neighbor might one day apply to hypothetical extraterrestrial life, just as it currently applies across national and cultural boundaries. Meanwhile, existential struggles—our sense of smallness or cosmic loneliness—can be met with pastoral care that anchors identity in a personal God who upholds galaxies and individuals alike. Worshipful awe, educational engagement, stewardship, and compassionate mission all converge to shape a church that beholds the night sky and glimpses the echo of divine artistry.

As believers live out their faith in this cosmic context, they embody a hopeful vision: that the God who authored the stars chooses to dwell with humanity, granting significance to each life and weaving the story of redemption through infinite spaces. In that confidence, the church can celebrate each new cosmic discovery not as a threat to faith but as an invitation to marvel anew at the Creator whose glory transcends both time and space. In so doing, we fulfill our role as stewards, worshippers, and bearers of hope in a universe that, in all its vastness, cannot contain the love of God.

Chapter 10: Are We Truly Alone?

From the earliest chapters of this book, we have recognized the age-old human longing to determine our status in the cosmos. Are we a solitary oasis of life in a vast and silent ocean, or are we one among many archipelagos of consciousness scattered among billions of stars? Ancient astronomers, theologians, philosophers, and even early Church Fathers wrestled with this question, albeit with limited observational tools. The modern era has provided us with telescopes, space probes, and a refined scientific method, propelling speculation about extraterrestrial life from the realm of myth and legend into mainstream inquiry.

Yet, even as exoplanet discoveries surge, and as cultural portrayals of contact with alien civilizations abound in fiction, the question "Are we truly alone?" remains elusive in both science and faith. It is not just a query for astronomers or theologians; it is an existential crossroads that touches identity, meaning, morality, and hope. In what follows, we will consider the significance of this question in four major themes: **(1) Integrating Insights from Biblical, Scientific, and Philosophical Explorations; (2) Lingering Questions and Christian Hope; (3) Living with Mystery and Wonder;** and

(4) A Vision for Future Exploration. Our goal is not to provide a definitive yes or no—indeed, such certainty does not yet exist—but to illuminate how the Christian faith can sustain believers, whatever cosmic realities may unfold.

10.1. Integrating Insights

10.1.1 The Tapestry of Biblical and Scientific Perspectives

Throughout this book, we have seen that neither Scripture nor science alone offers a conclusive answer about extraterrestrial life. The Bible reveals God's grand design for humanity's redemption on Earth (John 3:16), underscoring our unique role as bearers of the divine image (Genesis 1:26–27) and caretakers of the planet (Genesis 2:15). Yet, Scripture also portrays God as the Creator of "all things" (Colossians 1:16), a phrase that does not necessarily exclude living beings beyond Earth. Meanwhile, modern astronomy provides a glimpse into a universe seemingly large enough—and old enough—to host a multitude of potentially habitable worlds. Observational evidence for exoplanets has raised the probability (though not certainty) that life elsewhere may exist in microbial or even intelligent forms.

The tension between biblical specificity (God's revelation to humanity) and cosmic vastness (billions of galaxies) has prompted believers to ask whether the Earth story is but one chapter in a cosmic drama. Could God's plan encompass other rational creatures? Might the Incarnation of Christ (John 1:14) have implications for a galaxy we have never seen? These queries illustrate how scriptural and scientific vantage points can intersect without necessarily clashing. One may affirm the theological claim that humanity holds a special covenant relationship with God, while also acknowledging a divine prerogative to create wherever, and however, He wills. In such a tapestry, Earth's significance is not diminished by cosmic immensity; rather, it becomes a critical thread in a design that may extend far beyond our current scope.

10.1.2 Harmony and Humility in Our Cosmic Worldview

One common fear is that discovering alien life would unravel Christian doctrine. Yet, as we have noted, historic theological debates—whether about heliocentrism, the scope of redemption, or the nature of angels—demonstrate the Church's resilience in adapting to deeper understandings of creation. If conclusive evidence of alien life emerges, the Christian community might well undergo a period of robust discussion, drawing on its historical aptitude for theological reflection in new contexts. Indeed, many scholars propose that such a discovery would not negate the Incarnation or the Cross but might magnify God's creative and redemptive reach.

This calls for humility: an openness to the possibility that God's cosmos surpasses our expectations, and that the biblical narrative, while primarily focused on humankind, does not exhaustively catalog every manifestation of divine creativity. Therefore, any potential meeting with extraterrestrial beings, or simply continued speculation about them, should prompt believers to cultivate a posture that the Bible commends—"God opposes the proud but gives grace to the humble" (James 4:6). Genuine humility frees the Christian to celebrate new scientific discoveries as further chapters in the revelation of God's handiwork, even if they introduce complexities that demand fresh theological engagement.

10.1.3 Philosophical and Existential Dimensions

From a philosophical angle, the question of cosmic loneliness often leads to questions about purpose and meaning. If we are alone, does our uniqueness underscore a profound anthropocentric significance, or does it highlight our cosmic isolation? Conversely, if the universe teems with life, does that threaten our special standing, or does it suggest a grand communal tapestry where rational beings across the galaxies collectively reflect God's glory? The Christian worldview can accommodate both scenarios. Humans can retain uniqueness as the recipients of God's redemptive plan while acknowledging that God's freedom to create does not have to be restricted to Earth.

Existentially, the immensity of the cosmos may provoke awe or dread. Believers can interpret cosmic immensity as an invitation to worship, echoing the Psalmist's wonder: "When I consider your heavens… what is man that you are mindful of him?" (Psalm 8:3–4). Even if the cosmos reveals no other advanced civilizations, the sheer scale can cultivate humility and gratitude—a recognition that God, who upholds galaxies, also cares intimately for each human heart (Psalm 139:1–18). Such an existential anchor helps Christians navigate potential existential angst, focusing less on the question "Are we alone?" and more on the promise that God's presence pervades all creation (Jeremiah 23:23–24).

10.2. Lingering Questions and Christian Hope

10.2.1 The Silence and the Fermi Paradox

In scientific circles, one aspect of the question "Are we truly alone?" emerges from what is known as the Fermi Paradox: If intelligent life is common in the universe, why have we found no clear evidence or received no signals? Some postulate that civilizations may self-destruct before achieving interstellar outreach, others that advanced species might not desire contact, and still others that we have not looked in the right ways. For Christians, this silence could imply that Earth is indeed singular in harboring self-aware life. It might also mean that God, in His wisdom, has orchestrated a cosmos where contact is rare or delayed. None of these possibilities definitively contradict Christian teaching.

Biblically, one might liken the paradox to the notion of hiddenness—God sometimes seems silent in human affairs, yet faith affirms He is intimately active behind the scenes (Habakkuk 1:2–5). Could the cosmos mirror this dynamic, with life existing in ways not easily discernible? Possibly. The Fermi Paradox stands as an intriguing intersection of scientific logic and theological reflection: if the universe feels silent, does that equate to emptiness, or does it speak to a complexity we have yet to unravel?

10.2.2 The Reach of Redemption

A second lingering query concerns soteriology—if non-human, rational beings exist, how would redemption apply to them? From a Christian vantage point, many point to passages like Colossians 1:20, which speaks of Christ reconciling "all things, whether on earth or in heaven." Some interpret "all things" as inclusive of any alien life forms that might exist. Yet the Bible remains silent on the specifics of how that salvation might unfold outside the human context. The theological humility advocated throughout this book counsels us to hold this question with open hands, trusting that God's justice and love are not confined by our limited vantage point.

Would alien beings require their own Incarnation event? Could Christ's sacrifice on Earth be universally efficacious for them as well? These questions have no definitive answers in Scripture, so the Church can respond in a posture reminiscent of the early believers grappling with whether Gentiles could be part of God's covenant (Acts 10–15). The resolution then involved recognizing God's expansive grace. Similarly, if cosmic neighbors exist, the logic of God's redemptive love might extend beyond Earth in ways we cannot fully predict. What remains central is the anchor of Christian hope: Christ has triumphed over sin and death (1 Corinthians 15:54–57), ensuring that no dimension of creation is beyond the Creator's transformative reach.

10.2.3 Evangelism and Witness

A third question—especially in evangelical circles—concerns mission. If we discovered alien intelligences, should we attempt to "evangelize" them? In earlier chapters, we noted that Earth's Great Commission (Matthew 28:18–20) is specifically for humanity, though it has universal themes (Ephesians 1:10). The impetus for evangelism stems from a desire to share the news of redemption in Christ. Yet how that mission might apply to entirely different life forms, possibly unfallen or governed by distinct moral structures, remains speculative.

Some believers see no conflict in proclaiming Christ's cosmic lordship, while remaining open-minded about how or whether non-human beings might already know God in ways we cannot fathom. Others caution that an anthropocentric approach could be misguided. Ultimately, the impetus to share the gospel arises from love, not conquest or superiority. If cosmic neighbors exist, any outreach would require deep humility, respect, and an attempt to understand their unique spiritual context—just as effective cross-cultural missions on Earth demand learning local languages and customs. The call to love (John 13:34–35) would remain the foundational principle, guiding how believers approach the "other," whether earthly or extraterrestrial.

10.2.4 Ethical Stewardship on a Broader Scale

Finally, the question "Are we truly alone?" intersects with ethical concerns. Even if we never encounter alien life, the cosmic vantage reveals Earth as a singular habitat in an unfathomably large cosmos. This vantage invites us to reevaluate our stewardship responsibilities. Scripture consistently teaches stewardship rather than exploitation (Genesis 1:28, read in harmony with Genesis 2:15). Recognizing Earth's preciousness in a potentially vast but lonely universe can motivate Christians to champion environmental care, sustainable technologies, and peaceful global relations. If we do discover life elsewhere, ethical guidelines would be similarly crucial—prioritizing respect for other life forms, mutual learning, and the pursuit of peace (Romans 12:18).

10.3. Living with Mystery and Wonder

10.3.1 Embracing the Unknown

One thread weaving through each chapter of this book is the acknowledgment that many cosmic questions remain unresolved. Science offers hypotheses, Scripture provides spiritual frameworks, and theology explores possibilities, yet much about the universe remains mysterious. The psalmists repeatedly celebrate a God whose greatness is unsearchable (Psalm 145:3). In that spirit, living faithfully with cosmic questions entails embracing the unknown not as a failure but as part of the journey of faith.

For some believers, mystery can be unsettling, fueling anxiety or doubt. Yet a healthy biblical spirituality often thrives amidst partial knowledge (1 Corinthians 13:9–12). The same is true for cosmic speculation: we do not know for certain if aliens exist, how they would fit into salvation history, or whether the cosmic silence is absolute or temporary. Embracing mystery involves acknowledging these limits while remaining anchored in core convictions—God's love in Christ, the reliability of Scripture's moral and relational truths, and the abiding presence of the Holy Spirit (John 14:16–17).

10.3.2 Wonder as a Spiritual Discipline

A parallel attitude to mystery is wonder. Jesus Himself praised childlike openness (Matthew 18:3), a posture free from jaded cynicism, ready to marvel at the Father's works. Church history features saints and scholars—Augustine, Aquinas, Hildegard of Bingen, and others—who beheld creation with reverent awe. In modern times, the wonders of the cosmos can similarly drive believers to worship. Observing distant galaxies, pondering exoplanets, or contemplating universal constants can lead to gratitude for a Creator whose imagination surpasses our loftiest ideas.

Wonder can be cultivated through deliberate practices: reading Scripture with cosmic metaphors, engaging in prayer walks under the stars, designing worship services that highlight the magnificence of creation. Such practices do not require conclusive proof of alien life; they simply demand an openness to the grandeur that the cosmos reflects. This orientation counters the hubris that can accompany technological or scientific prowess. It reminds us that, as Job learned, we are finite participants in a creation that God alone fully comprehends (Job 38–42).

10.3.3 The Role of Community in Exploration

Christian tradition affirms that individual faith is nurtured within communal contexts (Hebrews 10:24–25). This principle applies to cosmic wonder as well. When believers gather to share insights, exchange doubts, and celebrate fresh discoveries, they create a supportive environment that balances imagination and accountability. The church as a community can serve as a "think tank" for cosmic reflection—organizing stargazing nights, hosting lectures by astronomers who share a faith perspective, and weaving cosmic themes into worship seasons.

Such communal engagement not only enriches personal devotion but also testifies to the broader society that Christians are not dismissive of knowledge. By modeling curiosity and reverence, the church can stand as a witness that faith does not fear scientific progress but approaches it with the humility of a disciple. This aligns with the biblical notion of the church as a "light to the world" (Matthew 5:14), shining not only through moral purity but also through an eagerness to learn and adapt under the Spirit's guidance.

10.4. A Vision for Future Exploration

10.4.1 Encouraging Responsible and Ethical Space Endeavors

As technology advances, humanity's footprint in space grows. Satellites fill Earth's orbit, private companies champion interplanetary travel, and international space agencies eye the Moon, Mars, and beyond. Christians can bring a moral voice to these ventures, advocating for responsible stewardship rather than unbridled exploitation. If the cosmos is ultimately God's creation (Psalm 24:1), venturing into space calls for an ethic that respects potential environments, prioritizes peaceful collaboration, and mitigates harmful impacts such as space debris.

Leaders in faith communities might consider forming committees or focus groups that track space-related developments and advise on ethical considerations. These groups could draw upon established Christian teachings on justice, stewardship, and human dignity, applying them in novel contexts like lunar mining or Martian colonization proposals. While the specifics remain emergent, the principle is clear: as we push further into space, a faith perspective can help guide decisions toward the common good, in line with biblical calls to love our neighbor (Mark 12:31) and preserve creation (Genesis 2:15).

10.4.2 Deepening Interdisciplinary Dialogue

The final chapter also offers an invitation for interdisciplinary dialogue. Scientists, theologians, philosophers, psychologists, and ethicists each bring valuable perspectives to the cosmic conversation. Collaborative gatherings, whether in academic conferences or local church forums, can yield fruitful cross-pollination:

- **Scientists** can share the latest research on exoplanets or cosmic phenomena.
- **Theologians** can reflect on scriptural and doctrinal implications.
- **Philosophers** can probe existential questions about meaning and value.
- **Psychologists** can address the emotional and mental impact of cosmic vastness or potential contact scenarios.
- **Ethicists** can propose frameworks to ensure that our cosmic endeavors align with principles of peace, fairness, and sustainability.

By pooling expertise, the faith community moves beyond superficial debates about "conflict between religion and science" and embraces a holistic exploration where synergy is possible. This synergy, in turn, can equip the Church for a future in which cosmic discoveries come faster, and the frontiers of knowledge expand daily.

Finally, this concluding vision emphasizes ongoing dialogue rather than a static resolution. Even if no definitive evidence of aliens emerges in our generation, the pace of scientific and cultural transformation ensures that the question "Are we truly alone?" will continue to shape hearts and minds. The Church, then, must remain flexible—rooted in the unchanging truths of the gospel while open to new contexts for application.

Practically, local churches and denominational bodies might integrate cosmic or creation-care concerns into their strategic planning, theological curriculum, and global outreach. Seminaries and Christian universities could revise curricula to include modules on science and faith that address cosmic realities in addition to terrestrial biological evolution or environmental ethics. Pastors might engage youth by connecting biblical themes of wonder to the latest images from space telescopes. Engaging these conversations with grace and depth can help believers remain relevant in societies increasingly attuned to cosmic questions.

Conclusion

This Chapter has sought to unify the threads woven throughout this book, reaffirming that the question "Are We Truly Alone?" cannot be answered with a simple yes or no. It remains an open inquiry—scientifically, as we lack definitive contact or detection, and theologically, as Scripture points both to Earth's unique role and God's boundless capacity to create. Rather than driving Christians to anxious speculation, this tension can become a wellspring of humble awe, moral reflection, and abiding hope.

For many, the cosmic perspective intensifies a sense of wonder: we stand on the threshold of a universe filled with potential marvels, each star and planet a testimony to divine creativity. Whether we ever confirm that life throngs distant worlds or find ourselves singular, we do not traverse this cosmic journey alone. Scripture attests that the One who "determines the number of the stars" (Psalm 147:4) also cares for the lilies of the field and the sparrows (Matthew 6:26–29). His attentiveness to the minutiae of our lives bridges the gulf between cosmic scale and personal significance.

Therefore, believers can rest in the assurance that, from a Christian standpoint, we are never truly isolated. God's presence pervades creation (Psalm 139:7–10), and the grace made known in Christ ensures a bond unbroken by distance or cosmic silence (Romans 8:38–39). The journey thus invites us to trust more deeply, love more generously, and steward our planet more faithfully. Whether or not cosmic neighbors exist, we carry the calling to reflect the Creator's compassion, to practice justice, and to proclaim the hope of resurrection within a universe that yearns for redemption (Romans 8:19–22).

In that sense, the final answer to "Are we truly alone?" extends beyond data or doctrine. It resonates in the believer's heart as a call to relational trust in God and loving engagement with fellow creatures. Whether we remain Earth's solitary watchers or someday discover cosmic kin, we can do so with the confidence that "in him we live and move and have our being" (Acts 17:28). This abiding promise fosters courage in uncertainty, peace in contemplation of the unknown, and above all, a radiant hope that the One who authors the stars also holds our future in His caring hands.